HENRY GORDON'S

WORLD OF MAGIC

HENRY GORDON'S
WORLD OF MAGIC

To Zita, Rita and Sandi,
who in the early days endured my endless exhortations
to "Take a card, any card!"

First published in 1989 by
Stoddart Publishing Co. Limited
34 Lesmill Road
Toronto, Canada
M3B 2T6

CANADIAN CATALOGUING IN PUBLICATION DATA

Gordon, Henry, 1919 -
    Henry Gordon's world of magic

ISBN 0-7737-2363-3

1. Conjuring. 2. Conjuring-History. 3. Gordon, Henry,
1919-   .
I. Title. II. Title: World of magic

GV1543.G67	1989	793.8	C89-094421-0

Excerpts appearing in Part III of this book are reprinted by
permission of the Toronto Star Syndicate.

Photographs: p. 6 - source unknown, from the collection of Henry
Gordon;   p. 25, 29, 42, 58 - from the collection of Henry Gordon;
p. 88 - publicity photograph (David Copperfield).

Illustration p. 71 - Sam Smiley (sketch donated to the author).

Cover Design: Linda Gustafson Book Design

Typesetting: Tony Gordon Ltd.

Printed in the United States of America

Contents

Introduction

When I decided to write this book I was immediately confronted with a problem — the problem of what to include and what to leave out. The conjuring art has so many facets that, in order to cover them adequately, one would have to write an encyclopedia of many volumes.

A survey of the magic books now on the market verifies this claim. There are books on the history of magic, on the lives of great magicians, on magic tricks for beginners, and on tricks for the more advanced. And there are books on the various magic specialties: card magic, coin magic, and mental magic; magic with sponge balls, with billiard balls, with ropes, with handkerchiefs, with thimbles, with newspapers, and on and on and on. There are books on magic for trade shows, for sales meetings, and for gambling demonstrations. There are books on magic-book collecting as a hobby. Need I say more?

Having been involved in this wonderfully crazy world of make-believe for almost half a century, and having soaked up a fair amount of experience and magical knowhow, I was tempted to cover the whole smorgasbord of prestidigitation. But rationality won out. I decided to zero in on a few areas that would really interest people who wanted more than a passing knowledge of the world of magic.

The reader I'm writing for is the person who is interested enough in the subject to want to know something of its history, of the giants who made modern magic what it is today, and who would like to acquire a repertoire of magical effects to get started in the world's greatest hobby. I hope that the section dealing with my own "world of magic" will also be of interest to the reader, dealing as it does with some of the magical "greats" I have encountered over the years, and describing the opportunities, the friendships, and the satisfaction one can derive from this amazing world which is known to very few.

I
My World of Magic

1
The Early Days

I can still remember the great magicians whose performances I witnessed when I was a youngster.

Howard Thurston at Montreal's Loew's Theatre. A Saturday, late morning. Two feature movies, various short subjects, and the fabulous stage show — admission 25 cents. Doesn't sound like much, but it was my week's allowance. However, if you brought a sandwich (no popcorn then) you could sit through the whole show again through the afternoon. No matter how many times we saw Thurston's miracles, we still couldn't figure them out. It must have been magic.

Then there was the Blackstone show. Harry Blackstone had not yet been placed on the public pedestal — that would happen only after Thurston retired — but to me, his show was another magical fantasy that had no equal.

Actually, the first magic act I ever witnessed was that of Hardeen, the brother of Harry Houdini. I was all of eight years old, and my mother had taken me to visit cousins in Atlantic City. The Steel Pier was the number one attraction at that resort, and Hardeen was its principal attraction that week.

I can still recall one of his unbelievable effects. He would pick up a number of large alarm clocks, one at a time, and cause each one to vanish, simultaneously making it appear again, hanging on a hook at the opposite side of the stage. The rest of his act seemed just as miraculous to an impressionable eight-year-old. But I came away from that particular show quite self-satisfied. I had figured it all out. What I had seen had not really happened. The magician had simply hypnotized the entire audience, myself included, into

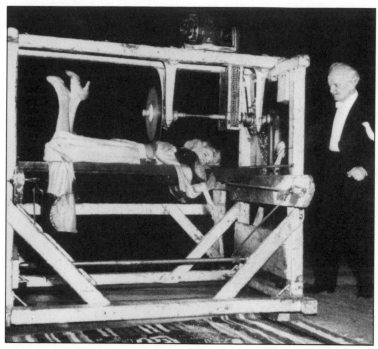

The Great Blackstone in action.

believing that these phenomena were happening. Nothing to it.

Now you might assume that, having seen these great magicians in action, I was inspired to emulate them and buy the first magic wand I could lay my hands on. After all, that's how most kids get bitten by the magic bug. Either that or they are hooked after receiving a magic set for Christmas or on a birthday. But for some reason these shows didn't affect me that way. Perhaps I was too busy with my stamp collection, my photography, my chess playing activities, my sports, or my developing interest in the opposite sex. Conjuring didn't enter into the scheme of things until the rather advanced age of twenty-one. Then it changed my whole life.

In 1940, with World War II upon us, I was serving as a wireless (radio) instructor in the Royal Canadian Air Force. My previous studies in that field had qualified me for the position. Canada, a safe haven, had been established as the base for the British Commonwealth Air Training Plan. Airmen from Britain, Australia, New

Zealand and South Africa were sent to Canada for their training before being dispatched to the war theaters.

Stationed initially at No. 2 Wireless School in Calgary, my duties were to train a rambunctious group of Aussies and New Zealanders in the fine art of radio communication before they went off to Gunnery school, and eventually graduated as Wireless Air Gunners, to assume that hazardous post in the Allied bomber fleets.

My days were busy, but the evenings were sometimes long and lonely — and boring. Boredom was the one thing I could not cope with. And still can't. But good fortune intervened. One day I was browsing in a downtown Calgary bookshop and spotted a small book on magic — coin manipulation, to be specific.

That book was the beginning, and I began practising right away. It wasn't easy, since I had no one to appeal to for assistance. And I badly needed help. You see, this was one of those magic books where the author had probably never performed any of the tricks he was describing. They just didn't work. The illustrations were fuzzy and the directions seemed to assume that I had six fingers on each hand.

But that didn't discourage me. The challenge was there. I simply bought another book, and then another. I was off and running. I was hooked. And when I began to perform some miracles for my students during off hours, I could see the payoff. My hard-bitten, cynical audience was impressed. My ego hit a new high. My self-confidence peaked. Where had this wonderful hobby been all my life?

After being transferred to No. 3 Wireless School in Winnipeg in 1941, I persuaded my one true love, Zita, to marry me, to leave Montreal and join me in Winnipeg, I had a new built-in audience — someone on whom I could inflict my new magical creations for an honest judgment. Through the years, her judgments have been nothing but tactfully honest, sometimes discouragingly so. But helpful? Yes.

I should hasten to add, after forty-eight years, that my addiction to conjuring was not the basic reason for my marriage proposal. But — an interesting aside — in all this time my patient spouse has never asked me to divulge the modus operandi of a trick. She feels that this gives her a better perspective on the viewpoint of the audience. Which doesn't mean that she hasn't spotted the occasional manipulative misstep that gave away what shouldn't have been given away. This is the way we learn.

After the war, back in Montreal, I discovered a world I had never been aware of: the magic shop and the magical fraternity.

In order to be a bona fide magician you had to have more under your belt than a few books and a somewhat limited knowledge of sleight-of-hand. There was also the financially draining necessity of acquiring magical props. One thing led to another. The yellow pages drew me to the downtown magic shop, and during the countless hours I spent browsing there I met other magicians who were immersed in the hobby. And that naturally led to my joining the local magic club. I was past the point of no return.

There is something obsessive about the practice of conjuring. Perhaps this stems from the desire to discover new ways to fashion puzzles. Or to hone the ability to solve them. Or to feel the self-confidence and satisfaction that you derive from being able to entertain others. In my case, it was probably a combination of all these things, in addition to the challenge that conjuring presented to my skills and intellect. And besides, after working all day in various branches of the electronics field, the change of pace was a great relaxant.

My family and friends were the first beneficiaries (victims?) of my new-found skills. I wouldn't dream of attending a social gathering without cramming my pockets full of magical artifacts. And it didn't take much coaxing to launch me into a full program of effects.

Probably the greatest failing of the beginning amateurs in this field is the conviction that they must display their entire repertoire at each performance. I was no exception to this rule. But, like others, I gradually learned better. Particularly when I noticed the odd yawn or the gradual drifting away of audience members to other rooms.

But there is really no better way to learn magic than by actually "magishing." And by listening to the advice of those able and willing to offer it.

My first venture into the field of professional conjuring was unexpected but rewarding. I had made the acquaintance of the manager of one outlet of the city's largest grocery chain. When he asked, "Would you like to do an act for our annual Christmas party?" I accepted, with trepidation. This would be my trial by fire. I would be paid. Twenty-five dollars. Cash. I had to measure up.

After hours of rehearsal, the big day came. The act went off without a hitch. They even applauded — with both hands. It wasn't until I got home that my heartbeat returned to normal and the dryness in my mouth disappeared. My professional career had been launched.

I do not exaggerate when I say that I was nervous. Until you have accumulated considerable experience, it can be traumatic to perform a magic act. You are striving to perform two contradictory feats at once. You are attempting to fool an audience and to entertain them at the same time. And it is doubly difficult for the neophyte — for a very good reason. You have not yet gained the confidence that comes with experience. The unseasoned performer knows how the secret moves are accomplished but is not yet quite certain if the audience can spot them or not. Have you really deceived them or is their applause merely polite? It takes many, many performances before the necessary confidence emerges.

And another thing. You cannot afford to make a mistake — any mistake. If you are a vocalist or a pianist you can hit a clinker and just carry on. It is soon forgotten. But if a magician errs during the middle of an effect — it all goes down the drain. The experienced professional soon learns to cover up and carry on, but for the beginner a slip-up can be shattering.

My career as a semi-professional magician began in the usual way: entertaining at children's birthday parties. First, I should perhaps explain the term "semi-professional magician." That means you're getting paid, but for God's sake, don't give up your regular job.

I would advise the reader not to downgrade the magician who performs at kids' parties. I know many a competent professional who has never had the nerve to do this. It takes skill, charm, tact, perseverance, a knowledge of child psychology, and above all, courage.

Courage? Well, after all, does the average night club, stage, or television conjurer have to compete with an audience that takes great delight in jumping up and searching the magician's pockets?

Or loudly and derisively explaining (even if usually incorrectly) how each trick has been accomplished? You learn to grin and carry on, patting each little tyke on the head while stifling the desire to throttle him. You might call it a baptism by fire — it really is.

But performing at kids' parties does have its compensations. There's the altruistic feeling you experience when you arrive and ring the front doorbell and the mother of the birthday child answers. Her hair is bedraggled, her mouth is twitching, her hands are shaking, and above the noise of mayhem in the background, you hear her say, "Oh, I'm so glad you're here."

I must admit, the little monsters in the audience are in a minority. Most of the kids really do enjoy a magic act if it is well presented. Many are not impressed with sleight-of-hand, but want to participate — that's the secret. They like nothing better than to have the magician ask them up to hold an article or do anything that will help to accomplish an effect. This assistant becomes a representative for the entire audience — a position of importance. So there is always a clamor by the youngsters, "Me, me, me!"

For me, conjuring for kids really was satisfying. Perhaps my greatest reward was seeing the look of wonder in their eyes after I had accomplished some apparently miraculous effect.

Perhaps the greatest compliment I ever received in my many years of performing was an indirect one made by a ten-year-old boy at the conclusion of my act. As he turned to his neighbor in the next seat I heard him say, "You know, I've changed my mind. I'm not going to be a doctor, I'm going to be a magician."

Entertaining at kids' parties was a learning experience for me. I got quite a good insight into the character and upbringing of individual children by observing their reactions. I also learned that adults, even if they sometimes won't admit it, are greatly intrigued by the art of legerdemain. At many of my performances the adults in the audience outnumbered the youngsters.

It took a couple of years to make the progression from living-room performance to the stage. I had done several tours of the wards at the Queen Mary Veterans' Hospital in Montreal, entertaining the hospitalized veterans, when the hospital's director asked if I would like to take part in a full-evening show being staged in the auditorium.

My first stage show — never to be forgotten. My first time in a spotlight — shattering. When I strode out on the stage, full of confidence, I was in supreme command. When the spotlight hit me, my confidence dissolved. The entire audience was wiped out — black. I couldn't see anything. I knew they were there — I could hear them breathing. But I had that awful feeling of speaking into nothingness.

Somehow I struggled through my routine and left the stage with an intense feeling of relief. I had reached another plateau.

Probably the greatest reward I garnered from my many years of magicmaking was the pure satisfaction I received from entertaining handicapped children. Usually sponsored by service organizations such as Rotary or Kiwanis, I made regular appearances at various summer camps and institutions in the Montreal area. Appearing at the Shriner's Hospital for Crippled Children was an annual event for me. These kids were a wonderful audience. Each trick brought forth enthusiastic applause. Their appreciation of my efforts was a pure delight. At the conclusion of my performance they would line up at the exit door, and an official would ask me to wait there. There they were, leaning on crutches or sitting on a wheelchair, some even lying on wheeled cots. Each would be brought up to me in turn, and thank me for the show. Scenes like that do not fade from memory.

The Institute for the Deaf was another regular booking. Here the principal of the school would stand beside me on the stage as I performed, using sign language to translate what I was saying to the audience. Here again the enthusiasm was inspiring.

Then there was the annual summer trip to the Retarded Children's Camp in the Laurentian Mountains, which I looked forward to as much as the kids. Amazingly enough, they would often remember tricks I had performed the previous year and ask me to do them again. And applause was not my only reward. These kids, more affectionate than most, would gather around me and give me great hugs and kisses.

It was always clear to me that handicapped children were my best and most appreciative audience. And the reason for that was easy to guess. These kids had been deprived of so much of the fun that normal children accept as a matter of course, that they took delight in any entertainment that came their way

One year I was invited by the B'nai B'rith organization to stage my magic act at the annual Christmas party of the huge St. Justine's Hospital for Sick Children in Montreal. For many Christmases, the party became an annual event for me. I was only one of the special features. The children also had the chance to meet some of the top players of the Montreal Canadiens Hockey Club, who circulated among them, handing out gifts, signing autographs, and spreading good cheer. After the party, the players and I always gathered in a nearby room to munch on cake and drink coffee. It wasn't long before I discovered that even hockey pros like a little hocus pocus.

So there I was, doing card tricks for Rocket Richard, Henri Richard, Bernie Geoffrion, Dickie Moore, Jean Beliveau, and the rest of that great championship team. The late, peerless goaltender, Jacques Plante, used to bring along his young son, sit him on his knee, and ask me to do something special for him. Judging by Jacques' reaction, he got just as much of a kick out of the magic as did the youngster.

As with any audience, I found it interesting to observe the reaction of the athletes to a conjuring performance. Most of them would gather around and take a keen interest in the proceedings. Others would pay little attention, as if it were beneath them to enthuse over such apparently childish activities. One team member, a journeyman player who spent only a year or two with the club (his name escapes me), turned out to be a magic enthusiast himself. He would grab some of my props and launch into a routine of his own. The players had a great time ribbing him on his efforts.

I suppose my greatest satisfaction came when, in subsequent years, I was asked by some of the team to magish for them again. Championship teams do have good taste.

During the 1950s I had the opportunity to bring my stage, or platform, act up to a more professional level. At that time the first large outdoor shopping centers were being built in Quebec. A well-known Montreal advertising agency had the contract for the public relations work for many of these centers. As each one opened, the agency would naturally plan an advertising blitz. I was lucky enough to have a good working relationship with these people, and they used my talents at most of the openings.

They would set up a platform on the open parking lot, with the usual awning, decorations and public address system. My act would be advertised, as would the names of some sports celebrities who would also make an appearance at the platform and sign autographs. Doug Harvey, the superb defenceman of the Canadiens, and Sam Etcheverry, legendary quarterback of the late, lamented Montreal Alouettes, often helped attract large crowds for my performances. It was great experience for me, and led to many other engagements.

One of these engagements, developed into a long-running booking which enhanced my image in the Montreal area — and gave me invaluable experience as a magician and an entertainer. I was asked to perform close-up magic for the patrons of Miss Montreal restaurant, one of the city's best-known dining spots. According to the initial booking I was to appear at the dinner hour every Thursday night for a period of three or four weeks, to see whether the act would catch on. I never did have a written contract, but the engagement stretched into several years. When the restaurant opened a branch at a suburban shopping center, I also entertained there on Tuesday nights. By this time I had acquired a professional tag line. I was advertised as Henry Gordon, The Great Pretender. I had no compunction about borrowing the name of that great musical hit by The Platters; their tune became an excellent theme song for my stage appearances.

At Miss Montreal, the evenings where I performed were known as Family Nights, and most of the tables were occupied by married couples and their children. So my legerdemain had to be slanted to please the adult and the youngster. Magic, of course, is one of the few entertainments that allow you to do this. I would approach each table in turn, trade some banter with the diners, then do a miracle or two, and move along.

After the first few weeks, management decided to add a new feature to Family Night. They partitioned off a large section at the rear of the restaurant and reserved it for kids' birthday parties — no adults were allowed in. They set up large tables, prepared a special menu, hung up balloons and decorations. A festive atmosphere prevailed.

Bookings were heavy. As far as the management and the guests were concerned, the venture was a complete success. As far as the waitresses and I were concerned it was one huge headache. We christened the back room "Riotville." Once free of parental control, the kids dropped all their inhibitions. Hot dogs would go flying through the air, waitresses would slip on ice cream dropped on the floor, tablecloths were doused with ketchup. The noise level approached that of a rock concert.

When I summoned up my courage and entered that perilous area I would be greeted by an ovation from all the tables, with loud entreaties to "come here first." I spent a few minutes at each table, performing two or three tricks, usually followed by calls of "More! more! more!" These shouts would be drowned out by shrieks from the other tables, "Come over here! Come over here!"

While all this was going on, some of the kids would be jumping up, shoving their greasy little hands into my pockets, looking for items which had previously vanished.

When I finally emerged into the front dining area, sweat dripping into my eyes, I was ready to burst into the manager's office and resign. But good sense prevailed, and I carried on by entertaining at the various tables in this section — to a civilized audience.

This type of entertainment is almost universal today, but in the fifties in Montreal, it was considered unique. I built up a considerable following, which again led to other engagements, and in some cases to friendships. But, best of all, I learned how important it is to make contact with and relate to an audience. Whether in magic or any other field, that is the true secret of success for an entertainer.

My television debut was probably one of the earliest in Canada. When television first appeared in this country, the Canadian Broadcasting Corporation was airing programs for just a few hours a day. Many of them were experimental, and all were live, usually covered by a single camera.

As president of the local chapter of the International Brotherhood of Magicians, I received a call from the CBC one day, asking if I could enlist a few magicians to do a show on air. We accepted with delight, planned a program, and presented it on the as-yet-unfamiliar medium. Memory fails me — the production may have been adequate, but I don't recall that we were asked back for a repeat performance!

It wasn't until 1956 that I got another opportunity to appear on the tube, but this was a biggie, a CBC network show called "Pick the Stars," broadcast out of Toronto. The program was elaborately produced, featuring a variety of performers each week. The top act would be called back to appear on another program later in the series. I was told by my family and friends (naturally) that I did well, but the act did not rate top billing.

My TV career in magic got rolling when I did a thirteen-week series on CBC's "Montreal Matinée," a highly rated afternoon magazine program. It was on this show that I introduced Henry Gordon's Kollege of Magical Knowledge, a feature I dreamed up in which I would highlight a different artifact on each show. For example, I would talk about coins and coin collecting, then close out by performing some conjuring with coins. Or I would demonstrate how different rope knots were used for various purposes, and then do a couple of rope tricks.

This series was followed by another called "Sandy and Company," in which I took second billing to a ventriloquist's dummy. Sandy was the dummy; I was the company. A talented young lady, Carolyn Blythe, was the ventriloquist. The formula we worked out was that I would perform the magical feats while a cynical Sandy questioned, derided, and lambasted everything I did. It didn't really bother me consciously, but I did finally devise a way to get my own back. On the last program of the series I had Carolyn place the little monster in a box, and I made him vanish, voice and all.

Those were my early days on television, when magic was my principal medium. Since then, right up to the present, I have appeared on hundreds of programs in Canada and the United States, but not strictly as a magical performer. I have expanded my horizons into exposing the flimflam used by so-called psychics and others who claim to have supernatural powers they do not actually possess.

But my conjuring powers still stand me in good stead, and I do use conjuring, particularly mind-reading effects, to punch home my arguments — and to entertain at the same time.

They said it couldn't be done. How can you perform magic on radio? Well, it could be done, and I did it. Not only did I do it, I taught it.

All this took place on a CBC Radio network program called "Is

Anybody Home?" which was probably the best radio program for young people that Canada ever produced. It ran for years and then died a natural death. Unfortunately for me, my segment died with it.

I had been teaching a course in magic for years, basically for adults. So when the producer of this program called and asked what sort of contribution I could make, the idea of teaching magic to young listeners immediately came to mind. We went ahead.

The presentation went this way: the young lady who hosted the program would introduce me. I would perform a trick for her, describing what was happening as I went along. It was completely spontaneous — she had no idea of what was going to happen. The listeners could hear her reaction. When the effect was completed, there would be a musical break, then we would come back and I would explain to her, and to the listeners, how the effect had been accomplished.

I had to choose my tricks with care. They had to be simple, easy to learn, and yet effective. The concept worked. Our mail indicated that we had developed a good following. I'll never know how many youngsters were encouraged to adopt this wonderful hobby as a result of the program, but there must have been quite a few.

Another CBC Radio series I performed in was the popular network show, "Morningside," with the host of the time, Harry Brown. That was back in 1977. For each program I would select a famous magician of days gone by and discuss his life and professional career. Again, the popularity of these broadcasts reflected the public's great interest in the ancient art.

One radio program I participated in had an unusual spinoff. It was a broadcast I did on CFCF-Radio, Montreal, in 1980. At that time I was featured on a one-hour-a-week open-line show on that station. I would have a ten-minute discussion with the show's host, after which the lines were opened and I would field questions from listeners.

On one particular day I was discussing the life of the great escape artist, Harry Houdini. Listeners were especially interested in the events leading to his death in 1926 because they had actually taken place in Montreal. I described that long-ago scene in Houdini's dressing room in the Montreal theater where two young men were witnesses to the blows being dealt the magician by a third party — blows which led to his demise.

When the phone lines were opened, the first call that came in was from a man with a deep voice: "Mr. Gordon, I heard your story about the death of Houdini. I thought you might be interested to know that I was one of the people in that dressing room."

Now, remember, this was fifty-four years after the event. And one gets many strange calls on open-line radio shows. I wasn't inclined to take it too seriously. However, I suggested that the caller stay on the line, that the producer would pick up his phone number, and I would call him back after the show.

When I returned his call, his responses to my questions made me take him a little more seriously. We arranged to meet, and when we did, the story I uncovered was intriguing. It also answered some lingering questions about Houdini's death. More about this in a later chapter, covering the life, and death, of Harry Houdini.

Professional magicians have many outlets for their craft. One of the more lucrative ones today is in the corporate field — the trade show and the sales meeting. At trade shows the magician is featured at the company booth, attracting and entertaining visitors and helping highlight the company's products. At the sales meeting magicians address the gathered salespeople, delivering the company message, using magical effects for dramatic impact.

At my first trade show appearance I realized that the immediate necessity was to catch the attention of the passing throngs. Here I was, standing behind a table in front of my sponsor's booth, a large sign announcing my appearance at various times during the day. The problem was that the passing throngs kept passing. I had to find a way to stop them.

I hit upon a method which I continued to employ for years. I used a trick in which a large handkerchief seemed to be suspended in midair without visible means of support. This illusion always managed to stop a few people who would come over to inspect it. Once I had their attention I would launch into my routine. And once this small group gathered, more people would join them, until the aisle was blocked — which would attract more spectators.

The people manning the adjoining booths would not be ecstatic about this traffic tieup, but who cared? My sponsor was happy.

For a number of years I concentrated on this field. It had its financial compensations and also presented a creative challenge. But the trade show circut is hard work, and inevitably results in burnout. I saw it coming — and quit.

When I first became involved in this branch of the magic field it was in its infancy, and the financial rewards were not as great as they are today. The average professional usually gravitated to the nightclubs. But today the clubs have more or less died out, and a good number of top pros have gone commercial. There is no other choice. Television work is fairly scarce, and staging the big full-evening magic show is no longer feasible, except for the very few with big names who can afford it.

For the young magician with good personality, adequate talent, and loads of energy and stamina, I would highly recommend the commercial magic field — if dollars are the main target.

If there was one thing that gave me tremendous satisfaction during my magic career, it was teaching the art to others. From the early 1970s until the late 1980s I conducted classes for groups of ten adults at a time. I got the idea after taking some individual lessons from a few of the real masters of magic in New York. But I decided to hold group sessions — in this way the fees could be kept much lower, and we could establish the kind of friendly atmosphere you find in a gathering where people have a common interest. It was gratifying to see how this course influenced some of its participants, who came from all walks of life. The majority were males, but there were several women, too. A number of my magical students occupied a high public profile, not for their conjuring abilities, but in other fields. Some were politicians, many were journalists, broadcasters, scientists. Others were professional people — doctors, lawyers, dentists.

I chose the curriculum with care. It's easy enough to teach a newcomer a few great tricks or to reveal some of magic's long-guarded secrets, but I decided to plant a foundation, so that those who were so inclined could go further in the art. So for every trick I taught, I explained the basic principle behind it. In this way the students could go on to inventing their own effects, which is the hallmark of the real magician.

With the multiplicity of magic books on today's market, there are literally thousands of tricks you can learn. But nothing can take the place of personal instruction. For every sleight-of-hand move you make, for every gesture, for every verbal remark during a presentation, there are a dozen ways you can do it wrong. Without correction by a competent instructor, you will just keep compounding your errors over the years. I've seen this happen countless times, particularly to amateur performers who become self-deluded to the point that they cannot see that they are doing anything wrong.

I always made it clear to my students that I was teaching magic, not necessarily as a career opportunity for them, but mainly as a hobby, a fun thing. But, as I'll point out later, this hobby can have many side benefits.

Some participants in the course went no further with their magical interests. They had probably joined the group simply out of curiosity. I could spot them during the sessions. They were interested in the modus operandi of the tricks, but spent little time on practice. But others really got hooked. I ran into some of them in later years at magic conventions in the United States.

Still others put their new-found magical knowledge to more practical use. There was the life insurance salesman whom I encountered about a year after his "graduation," who informed me that his business had boomed since he had become a magician. "How so?" I asked, knowing what his answer would be. "Well," he said, "I usually visit my clients at their homes in the evening. Now, before I leave my office, I stuff my pockets with magic tricks. At the client's home, instead of pulling out my sheets of statistics and going into a sales pitch, I first greet his kids, then sit them down and do a fifteen-minute magic act. The whole family gets into the spirit of the thing. By then I've broken down the barriers, and I'm talking to a friend instead of to a sales-resistant skeptic."

One of my early students was a super enthusiast. A topnotch, highly paid salesman in the garment trade, he gave up his whole business, moved to Florida, and opened a restaurant featuring magical entertainment. The last I heard, he was doing extremely well.

I wasn't in the habit of asking my students why they were taking a course in magic. But I did wonder what had motivated some of them. One who'd had me puzzled gave me a pleasant surprise. He was a professor of architecture at a Montreal university — a gentleman well along in years. When he came to the final session, he came up to me with a pleased smile on his face and said, "You should be very proud of me." I asked what he meant. He explained: he had taken the course for one basic reason. He had just returned from Ottawa, where he had attended the birthday party of one of his grandchildren. But he had not been just a guest. He had been the star of the show — a performing magician! "You know, Mr. Gordon," he said, "I have written several textbooks on architecture and hundreds of papers on the subject. But nothing has given me greater pleasure than this opportunity to be a hero to my grandchildren and their friends."

I now know exactly what he meant. After many, many years of retirement from the birthday party scene, I am once more in demand for appearances at *my* grandchildren's birthday parties. And I am something of a hero in *their* eyes. You just can't beat that kind of satisfaction.

One dentist who took my course put his newly acquired conjuring capabilities to good, practical use. Whenever he got a nervous youngster on the chair, he would trot out a quick trick before inflicting the necessary torture. This, he told me, was a very effective way of helping the quaking patient relax.

One well-known gentleman took my course: Terry Mosher, better known as Aislin of the Montreal *Gazette*. Terry is one of the leading political cartoonists in Canada, and famous all over the continent. His cartoons appear not only in the *Gazette*, but also in news publications throughout North America, and he has had several books of cartoons published. Terry told me right off the bat that he was interested only in card tricks. So he attended only those sessions which included that branch of the art, and I managed to squeeze in a few extra private card sessions with him. I sometimes wonder if he still continues his chicanery with cards.

Some people signed up for the course with trepidation. I remember the truck driver who said, "How can I do magic with these thick fingers?" He soon learned that there are many other tools in a magician's repertoire: apart from sleight-of-hand, the performer can use subtlety, psychology, ingenious artifacts.

Several years after I had begun this course I contacted as many of my ex-students as I could reach and organized a reunion party. It was a tremendously successful evening, as they brought along their spouses and friends, and performed for them in a full stage show that I had organized. For me, the high point of the evening occurred when one of the women came onstage and did an excellent ten-minute routine. I was sitting at a table with her husband, who happened to be an acquaintance of mine. When she began to perform he almost fell off his chair. He turned to me and stuttered, "My God, I didn't know she could do that. I thought she brought me here tonight because we know you." "But didn't you know she was coming to my classes every week?" I asked. "No, she said she was taking a sewing course."

One group of students I taught had special reasons for learning conjuring. They were patients convalescing in Montreal hospitals, where I taught magic, using the art as a form of therapy. I designed a series of simple tricks to help improve the patients' dexterity, visual perception, coordination, and cognitive skills — and most of all, to improve self-confidence and build self-esteem. Those people would include those who had suffered strokes and had the motor functions of their hands impaired. The practice of simple sleight-of-hand helped greatly in their rehabilitation. After I worked with the patients, I taught these tricks to therapists, who would then take over.

Programs like this now exist in some institutions in the United States. There should be more of them.

Blackstone's famous autographed self-portrait

2
The Fraternity

B eyond the everyday, workaday world there exists a magical realm that most people are not aware of. No, it's not the mythical world of J.R.R.Tolkien. It's the guarded, shadowy, but actually quite accessible world of the magical fraternities.

In 1951, after eleven years as an amateur and semi-professional magician, I stepped into another world by joining Ring 62, the Montreal chapter of the International Brotherhood of Magicians. At that time, the requirements for being accepted as a member were a little more stringent than they are now. You had to do a magic act for a very critical audience, consisting of Ring members who were quite particular when it came to accepting new members.

There is no substitute, however, for belonging to this type of organization. Like many other magicians who joined these magical clubs as neophytes in the art, I found membership to be a decided asset. When I first joined IBM's Ring 62, I met other magicians, learned from them, formed new friendships, and expanded my horizons. As a member, you find yourself benefiting from the support of your colleagues and giving them support as well. A whole new vista opens up. The world of magic is yours for the taking.

The International Brotherhood of Magicians (IBM), with more than twelve thousand members in over fifty countries, is one of the two great magic organizations in the world. The other is the Society of American Magicians (SAM).

The International Brotherhood of Magicians was formed in 1922 when two young prestidigitators, Len Vintus of Winnipeg, and

Gene Gordon of Buffalo, decided to organize a small correspondence society in which people interested in magic could exchange ideas. The original headquarters was in Winnipeg, but as the society grew it was shifted to Kenton, Ohio. The original members could not have dreamed that their small group would develop into the huge organization it has become, with thousands of members all over the world.

As the membership increased, rings were established in various cities, each one with its own number. There are now more than two hundred rings in the IBM, including Ring 269 in Harlingen, Texas. That location may not sound very exotic, but how about Ring 264 in Pardess-Hana, Israel; Ring 148 in Adelaide, South Australia; Ring 204 in Rome, Italy; Ring 207 in Lausanne, Switzerland; Ring 67 in Bombay, India; Ring 190 in Nice, France; Ring 182 in Buenos Aires, Argentina; and Ring 231 in Yokohama, Japan. And, of course, there are rings in almost every major city, (and in some not so major ones), in the United States and Canada. Ring 25, the British Ring, is the largest of all. It includes members from all over the United Kingdom.

All members of the IBM receive its superb monthly publication, *The Linking Ring*. The title is quite appropriate, because the magazine helps link together the rings from around the world. And, of course, if you've seen just a few magic acts, you must have already been intrigued by the linking ring routine in which the conjurer makes several large, solid steel rings magically link and unlink.

If most magicians are like me, the first thing they do when they get their copy of The Linking Ring is read the ads. They're enough to make any magician's mouth water. Of course, every magic dealer claims that the latest magical invention is a miracle maker. It takes more than a little experience in the art to separate the wheat from the chaff, but all the ads make for fun reading. They describe the effect that a particular trick will achieve, so for years I've exercised my magical imagination by trying to figure out the method which would accomplish each particular effect. This in itself is a stimulating part of the hobby.

Then the magazine carries its regular columns and feature articles by well-known magical writers, with the latest magic news and views. The back section features "Ring Reports," which have been sent in from rings around the world, reporting on local magical events and meetings. Each report is headed by the name and address of the ring's president and secretary, which provides an invaluable service. For example, whenever an IBM member is visiting a city in his travels he can contact a ring officer in advance. Almost invariably the welcome mat is put out for the visiting magi by the local members. My wife and I have enjoyed this hospitality many times over. One member of the Hawaiian group used to meet visiting magicians at the Honolulu airport and drape leis around their necks as they stepped off the plane.

To active magicians, the most popular feature of *The Linking Ring* is the Hocus Pocus Parade. This is an entire section containing instructions on performing the latest magical miracles dreamed up by contributing members. This section alone makes each copy of the magazine a collector's item — one reason why very few members will discard their back issues. I am a living example of that, holding every issue I have received since I first joined the IBM. That's a pretty high stack of magazines in the closet — among the stacks of other magical magazines, of course.

The Society of American Magicians, the oldest magical society in existence, was organized in 1902 in the famous Martinka Magic Shop in New York City by twenty-four men. They met in a little room at the back of the shop. The SAM chapters are called assemblies, and the first one was founded in San Francisco in 1917. There are now well over one hundred assemblies in the United States, Canada, and abroad. The SAM's journal is *M-U-M*, which stands for Magic, Unity, Might. Harry Houdini was one of the SAM's earliest presidents.

The SAM and the IBM are set up according to similar rules. To be a member you have to have an interest in magic, and you need some experience in the field, either as a performer or as a participant in the hobby. Two sponsors are usually required. And each member must take an oath of secrecy, to protect the basic principles of the ancient art. More on that controversial subject later.

There are several professional magicians in these societies, but the bulk of members are semi-pro and amateur performers. A good many do not perform magic at all — they may be magic collectors, bibliophiles or merely interested observers of the magical scene.

*The Great Blackstone creates his napkin rabbit for members of Montreal's
Ring 62, International Brotherhood of Magicians (the author is seated at
his right).*

When I first joined Montreal's Ring 62 in the 1950s, nightclubs were flourishing in the city, and many of them featured top magicians. Whenever a magic act came to town, a number of our ring group would attend the performance, and then invite the prestidigitator to the home of one of the members. My own home became a regular meeting place after the performer's last show, which would sometimes close around midnight. Imagine this scenario: an internationally known conjurer sitting in your living room with about half a dozen engrossed magical enthusiasts, exhibiting some of his pet magical effects until four o'clock in the morning.

Magicians like Del Ray, Roy Benson, Hen Fetsch, Al Wheatley, and Harry Blackstone lit up our magical scene. Many of these magicians never did become household names — except Blackstone, of course — but as entertainers they were always highly rated on any program.

Del Ray, still active, was a pioneer in using electronics to accomplish his miracles. Now his act is polished to perfection. Roy Benson who specialized in comedy presentations, was one of the greatest in that field. Hen Fetsch, a personal friend who died at too early an age, was one of the greatest inventors of magical effects. Many of his creations are still in great demand in the magic marketplace. I can still remember him sitting on a couch with me, picking up a coin and a handkerchief, and immediately devising a knockout effect — with the coin visibly penetrating the centre of the hanky and then changing into a different coin.

Al Wheatley, a world-traveling performer who wore oriental garb and makeup for his act, was known professionally as Chop Chop. At our invitation, Al once attended a Ring 62 meeting and did a special show while he was between performances at a local club. You must remember that when a magician performs for other magicians he always strives for that little extra something that will deceive even the knowledgeable ones. Well, Al Wheatley was no exception. He drove us silly with one particular effect. With his back turned, he directed me to place a wadded-up dollar bill under one of three inverted teacups. He then asked me to move the cups around as much as I wished. Then, turning around, he immediately pointed to the cup that was covering the bill. And he was right. He then broke a primary rule of magic. He repeated the effect. We were still stymied.

After Al left to get back to the club, we spent the rest of our meeting trying to figure out this puzzler. No success. The meeting broke up. On the way home, I stood at the corner of Peel and St. Catherine Streets for almost an hour with two of my magical buddies, arguing with them about various methods Wheatley might have used. Still no satisfaction. We headed off in different directions.

When I got home it was after midnight. Zita was fast asleep. I made for the kitchen. Now most normal people would have probably headed for the refrigerator at this point. Not me. I went to the cupboard, removed three cups, sat down at the table, wadded up a piece of paper, and began thinking.

It must have been two in the morning when I hit pay dirt. I got it. The next step was the usual one: I had to try it out on someone. No problem. I strode into the bedroom and gently wakened Zita. "Come on into the kitchen. I've got a great effect to show you."

This may sound exaggerated, but I swear it's true. She did not get violent — she merely complained mildly, got up, donned a robe, and staggered after me. Spouses of magicians do get that way. They become indulgent, sympathetic, understanding, fatalistic. Some say they have to be that way if they want to hold the marriage together.

I did fool her with the effect, and I've used it many times since. As a little bonus to my readers I've included it in the "Magic for Everyone" section of this book. And I have credited it to the actual inventor of this clever conceit.

I would highly recommend anyone involved in the hobby of conjuring to join a magical society. You will meet the most interesting people — and you can catch up on your sleep in later years.

3
The Conventions

The first convention I ever attended as a magician was also probably one of the greatest and most star-studded gatherings ever held. The earliest such meetings were annual events, held separately by the SAM and the IBM in the United States. But this one was a combined IBM-SAM shindig. The year was 1951; the place, the old Commodore Hotel, next to Grand Central Station in New York City. The two societies had pooled their resources to get the best in magical entertainment — and they certainly succeeded.

For me, new in the fraternity but well read in the history of magic, this gathering was a revelation. Wherever I turned, in the lobbies or the reception rooms, I came face to face with some of the great names in magic, past and present. I spoke to and photographed conjurers I had long read about but never expected to meet. To see some of them perform on stage and in close-up sessions was just icing on the cake. I've attended dozens of conventions since that time, but none was as memorable as that one.

I've often been asked the question, "What do magicians do at a magic convention?" Well, here's the answer.

They meet other magicians they haven't seen for perhaps a year or more, compare notes, talk over old times, and trot out their newest conjuring creations. For there's nothing a magician enjoys more than baffling another magician. Some of these sessions go on during the day, some take place in the evening, and others take you well into the night. If you attend a gathering of magicians don't bother to pack your pyjamas — you won't be needing them.

Perusing any convention's printed program, you will notice that very little time is allotted for rest, or even for meals. From early in the morning to late at night the structured schedule is packed with events. The daylight hours are taken up with lectures by noted magicians, who reveal many of their effects and teach proper presentation. There are special events and lectures for the magicians' spouses. Then there are the close-up sessions, where the magician sits at a table, performing with cards, coins and other small props, while the audience is seated near the table, usually in tiered rows of seats.

In the evenings the big stage shows are featured, either in the hotel auditorium or in a nearby theater. Here the big acts perform under more than the usual pressure. They're working for a discerning audience, many of whose members know the secrets of most effects. So the magician on stage is always looking to produce a new effect, or a new wrinkle on an old effect.

The featured acts at the 1951 convention were a Who's Who of the top magicians of the day. Milbourne Christopher, author and master magician, who staged a rare Broadway magic show, MC'd the first evening. Al Flosso, known as the Coney Island Fakir, convulsed the audience with his hilarious act. (I have much more to tell about Al later on.)

The author in the lobby of New York's Commodore Hotel, for his first magic convention in 1951.

Francis Carlyle was on the bill, as well. Francis was famous among magicians as one of the world's greatest experts in card magic. I was fortunate to be able to take a few lessons from him in my earlier days, but would never dream of approaching his level of skill. At this convention he stunned the audience by walking into the wings on one side of the stage and then reappearing, in a split second, on the other side — then repeating the miracle. It wasn't until the next day that someone who knew Carlyle well revealed to me that he had a brother who was an identical twin.

After the evening show at these conventions most of the attendees head for the dealers' room. Here the magic dealers from many countries display the latest gimmicks and magical effects on the market. And here, a magician and his money are soon parted. Most devotees of conjuring are a soft touch when it comes to buying magic tricks. They'll buy anything in sight. And it usually ends up in a closet in a magic den, unused, often not even unpacked. These are what I call "the toys of the trade." No problem. It keeps you young at heart.

Another magical memory emerges out of the mists.

It was early on a Sunday morning — a sunny fall day in New York's Catskill mountains in 1985.

As I picked my way through the huge lobby of Brown's Hotel I surveyed a scene I've witnessed many times: here and there a discarded deck of cards — a few people reclining on the lounges in a semi-stupor.

No, it wasn't the end of a boozing and gambling weekend — it was the tail end of a magicians' convention. The exhausted survivors had just concluded an all-night session of miracles, trying to deceive their fellow conjurors. A typical scene at the close of many a magicians' bash.

This particular convention had been founded in the sixties by Louis Tannen, head of the world's largest magic supply company, Louis Tannen Inc. of New York. The Magic Jubilee became an instant success, with an average of 1,300 now attending each year. Louis Tannen, an old friend, has since passed on, but his successor, Tony Spina, has carried on the tradition at Brown's.

Many magic conventions are held each year, but the Jubilee has a flavor all its own. It's the only magical gathering where the registrants sleep under one roof, have their meals together, and enjoy a beautiful rural setting. Brown's, one of the most renowned of the Catskill hostelries, is the spot where Jerry Lewis started out as a busboy and went on to become one of America's top comedians.

The Jubilee has always attracted some of the top names in showbiz — as performers and as registrants. Among those I have met in past years are Muhammad Ali, Dick Cavett, Johnny Carson, and Henny Youngman. The late Orson Welles, an accomplished magician, tried to come during the last couple of years of his life, but couldn't fit it into his schedule. Ironically, it was at the 1985 Jubilee that Welles's death was announced.

At the same Jubilee I met another suave and charming gentleman — Franco Contiglioni, a leading architect from Rome, Italy. Bitten by the magic bug, he told me he was giving up his profession to open a magic shop in Rome. You would have to be a magician to understand his motivation.

I also ran into an old acquaintance, Larry Weeks, who is unknown to most of the present generation. But Larry was once a big name in showbusiness — the top juggler in America. Probably one of his greatest achievements was teaching *me* how to juggle — at another convention some years back. I should explain: in the entertainment field, jugglers and ventriloquists are the magicians' cousins. They often attend each other's conventions.

Here too I met Harry Lorayne — magician, author, and one of the world's leading experts on memory systems. Harry has written several books on memory and has been running courses on the subject for years. Once again he had forgotten my name.

Several years later, I met Harry again on a television program in the New York area. Did he remember my name? You guessed it.

The three evenings of the Jubilee always feature well-staged magic shows in the ornate Jerry Lewis Theater Club. Each year Tony Spina combs Europe, the Orient, the United States, and Canada for fresh magical talent, and always seems to come up with winners.

Many now-famous magicians were first showcased at the Jubilee — among them David Copperfield, who received a standing ovation from over a thousand magicians in his debut.

At the 1985 gathering, illusionist Andre Kole wowed the audience when he caused a woman, lying prone, to shrink visibly until she was about two feet long. Fortunately, she grew back to her original size in a few seconds. The thing was astounding, even to experienced magicians.

The Pendragons, a male-female team from Las Vegas, brought down the house with a series of superb, fast-moving illusions and escapes. This team is now one of the most dynamic and sought-after magic acts on the scene.

But as with most magic conventions, the real action began after the evening shows. The informal magic sessions went on well into the night.

Friday afternoon found a large audience at poolside on the outdoor patio. Yogano, a middle-aged inventor of magical illusions who had just flown in from France, was about to display one of his original miracles.

He stood beside a small table. His attractive daughter was "hypnotized," placed on her back on the table, and the table then removed. There she remained, suspended in mid-air in front of the magician, with no visible means of support. In broad daylight. With the audience standing all around them. A knockout!

To me, the greatest fun at a Jubilee is dining, ten to a table, in the vast dining room. Before long, the cards and the coins are out, the food is ignored, the prestidigitation begins. Magicians table hop to show their latest creations. The waiters forget to serve dessert — they're standing around watching the miracles, their eyes bulging out. This Jubilee was no exception.

It all wound up on Sunday morning, with me wandering about the lobby in a euphoric state of semi-exhaustion — a typical wind-up for a magic convention.

4
Magical Meanderings

My career in magic has led me down many strange pathways. I have met people I would not otherwise have encountered in a single lifetime. I have visited places on two continents that I would not have likely seen, and I have had unusual experiences that have added the flavor that makes life worthwhile.

I can recall the time I took part in a theater variety show at one of the annual winter carnivals at Sir George Williams University in Montreal. On the program, among others, were two great showbiz stars: the late, great folksinger, Josh White, and none other than Milton Berle. Uncle Miltie happened to be in town, performing at the El Morocco nightclub, and had condescended to make a brief appearance onstage to crown the carnival's Coronation Queen. No doubt this helped to pack the theater.

While the show was in progress and I was standing in the wings waiting to go on, I noticed Berle standing nearby. Spotting my magic props beside me, he sidled over and asked, "You're a magician?" I nodded nervously — nervous because I was suffering the usual pre-performance jitters and because the great man himself was talking to me. "Do you have a deck of cards?" he continued. Again I nodded. "Gimme them, gimme them, I'll show you a trick," barked Berle in his usual staccato manner.

At this point I should explain: Milton Berle is one of the many prominent showbusiness personalities who have adopted magic as an avocation. To name just a few: Mickey Rooney, Orson Welles, Tony Curtis, and the silent movie great, Harold Lloyd. There are many others.

Well, when Milton Berle grabbed the pack of cards I offered

him, everyone backstage gathered around, and he proceeded to do a "trick" that left me singularly unimpressed. He had someone select a card, look at it, remember it, and hand it back to him. Whereupon Berle tore the card up into tiny pieces, tossed it over his head, and shouted, "Happy New Year" The backstage audience was amused — I was disappointed. I had been expecting some clever sleight-of-hand from Berle. I realized later that he was merely illustrating the first rule of showbusiness — *entertainment* comes first.

By the way, Berle had made it clear that his onstage appearance would be brief, that he would crown the queen, say a few words, and exit. Well, once he got on stage they couldn't get him off. Typical Milton Berle. But it was a great bonus for the audience. I was fortunate that my act didn't follow his directly. It would have died.

During the 1950s The Great Blackstone made several appearances in Montreal with his marvelous touring extravaganza. During one of these visits, in 1955, I met him at his hotel one afternoon and conducted him to a nearby restaurant where members of our magic club had gathered to honor him as our luncheon guest.

Harry Blackstone, one of the greatest professional magicians of the century, was one of the most genially cooperative when it came to meeting local amateur groups. He thoroughly enjoyed demonstrating impromptu magical effects for anyone willing to watch. He was always the magician, onstage or off.

This particular afternoon was no exception. He was more than generous in performing for us at the table and in regaling us with anecdotes of his lifetime in magic. As usual, in this sort of situation, most of the restaurant staff gathered around, and service to the other diners came to a standstill.

After Blackstone's theater performance that evening, a few of us picked him up backstage and headed for my home, where the magical festivities continued. I managed to whip out my trusty 8-mm movie camera and photograph Harry doing an astounding effect. He held a glassful of wine in front of him, only to have the contents of the glass vanish suddenly and mysteriously. To this day I have not admitted that I used "stop photography" to create this miracle. Why ruin two reputations — his and mine.

Harry Blackstone's performance in the Montreal restaurant brings back memories of another restaurant, in another year, in another city far removed from Montreal — Naples, Italy.

In 1970 Zita and I were enjoying our first really long vacation together, touring Britain and the European continent. Once in Rome, we could not resist visiting Naples, and its outlying attractions, the Isle of Capri and of course, Pompeii.

In Naples, we met an American couple and adjourned with them to a restaurant for dinner. The place we chose was one of the larger and more popular dining places, situated at the edge of the Bay of Naples. Our table partners, learning that I was a magician, naturally asked if I would do a trick or two for them. After dessert I was only too glad to oblige, having, by chance, a deck of cards in my pocket. Now, all during dinner the usual strolling musicians — in this case three guitar players — had been moving from table to table. When they came to our table and saw the hanky panky going on, a strange thing happened. They laid down their guitars, gathered round, and watched my shenanigans. After a few minutes one of them yelled out something in Italian to the rear of the restaurant. In a few more minutes the chef, his helpers, and others of the staff came out and joined our audience.

The payoff came when our waiter, who had been very discreet up to that point, suddenly whipped a coin out of his pocket and went into a routine of sleight-of-hand, then asked for my approval of his technique. No question, magic is the international language.

It was during this sojourn in Naples that I had a most unexpected experience — an unscheduled magical performance for a distinctly non-average audience.

Mike Rogers, born in Wyoming, and now residing in San Diego, California, is a very personable and accomplished magician. I had met Mike in the 1960s when he was a featured performer at a big magic convention in the United States. I had heard that Mike, who was an air traffic controller in the U.S Navy, was now stationed at NATO headquarters in Naples. So when we were in Rome, and preparing to depart for Naples, I called him and arranged to meet. He insisted on setting up our hotel accommodations and asked Zita and me to keep our first evening in Naples open.

It turned out that Mike, who was a pretty active guy, doubled as night manager for the Officers' Club at NATO headquarters. And that's where he and his wife drove us on our first night in the southern Italian city. The club was nothing if not luxurious. It had everything: sports facilities, swimming pool, bowling alley, and a nightclub as large and ornate as you would see anywhere. Every night there was a full orchestra and a different floorshow.

After the four of us had finished dinner and the floorshow had ended, at Mike's suggestion we moved to a larger table, where we were joined by several gentlemen in uniform. I believe the lowest-ranking officer at the table was a colonel. They were from the armed services of Greece, Turkey, Italy and other NATO nations.

After introductions, Mike turned to me and said, "You know, Henry, they've seen me do my stuff many times. How about showing them some Canadian magic?" Would it have been polite to decline? And besides, the cards in one pocket, the small sponge balls in another, and the Canadian half-dollars in still another were doing no good just lying there.

So there I was, sitting at a table in Naples in April 1970, doing my thing for a group of high-ranking NATO officers. It revived memories, memories of doing my first shaky magic routines in 1940 for the Aussies and New Zealanders stationed in Calgary.

Today, Mike Rogers, retired from the Navy, is one of America's busiest magic performers on the lucrative trade show circuit, and still entertains at magic conventions. I hope our paths will someday cross again.

For many years while we lived in Montreal, Zita and I made regular motoring trips to New York City. At first we went to visit friends and relatives, to sightsee, and to enjoy the theater and museums. Then, when the magic mania really took hold of me, these visits took on a new meaning and became even more frequent.

During the day, Zita would shop and visit the museums and art galleries, while I made a beeline for some of the Big Apple's famous magic shops. My favorite, and the only major one that has survived in New York from the early days, was the emporium presided over by Louis Tannen. Lou had gone through all the early business struggles, running novelty shops, but always carrying a line of magic tricks — until he finally concentrated on magic alone and built a business now acknowledged to be the largest magic dealership in the world.

Once into magic, Tannen decided to concentrate on customers who were basically magicians. So he located his shop on one of the upper floors of a 42nd Street office building, thereby avoiding casual street trade. From there he moved to larger quarters on Broadway, above the Loew's State Theater. Apart from his store trade he built a huge mail-order business, which became the real foundation of the establishment. He also branched out as one of the largest publishers of magic books, wholesaling his books and his magic tricks to other dealers around the world.

It was in the 42nd Street shop that I, among many other amateurs, learned what conjuring was really about. I would watch Lou and some of his able assistants demonstrating tricks for the customers. I would meet other magicians, amateur and pro, who were generous with their advice and captivating with their magical anecdotes.

And the prominent personalities I met at Tannen's made each visit a little adventure. Walter B. Gibson, Houdini's biographer, and the writer who created that fabulous fictional character, The Shadow, was a frequent visitor. I can still remember the Saturday afternoon he joined a few of us at a nearby restaurant for coffee and conversation. Gibson was a walking encyclopedia on magic and great magicians of the recent past, most of whom he had known personally.

It became a Saturday afternoon ritual for a small group to adjourn to that particular restaurant. There I met and got to know so many leading magical figures of the day — Martin Gardner among them. Martin is, of course, known today as a leading mathematician, philosopher, science writer, puzzle expert, and author. What many people don't know is that he has been a magician and magical writer for many years. Indeed, self-effacing as he was, in those days I knew him only as a magical enthusiast. He never spoke of his other talents. Today, as Fellows of the Committee for the Scientific Investigation of Claims of the Paranormal, he and I share another common cause.

Then there was Richard Himber. Now, Himber is a name that will mean absolutely nothing to many people today. But back in the days when big bands were all the rage in popular music, Richard Himber was a major name. For years before the advent of television, his orchestra was featured on some of the major radio network shows.

When I first met him at Tannen's in New York, I wondered what this famous musician was doing in a magic shop. I soon found out. Himber's principal hobby was magic. Not performing — inventing. He specialized in devising magical props that were sophisticated, clever, beautifully constructed — and expensive. Most of them were quite different from the usual magical paraphernalia, which were often garishly painted and hokey. His items seemed to be ordinary, everyday articles. For example, there was the Himber Wallet, still on the market, and one of several of my treasured Himber props. The Wallet is handsome, well constructed of quality leather, and it can be used as an ordinary billfold. On the other hand, it can also be used to perform some very clever deceptions.

Himber enjoyed selling his goodies directly to magicians instead of distributing them to retailers. I was a direct beneficiary of this policy, once he got to know me. Whenever I'd meet him during a New York visit, he'd grab me by the arm and say, "C'mon, let's go over to my place, I've got something new you'll like." He'd hail a cab and we would take off for his residence, an apartment at the plush Essex House bordering Central Park.

Richard Himber was no shrinking violet. He was brash, assertive and provocative — and a hard-sell salesman. Many in the magical community disliked him for these qualities, but I discerned a heart of gold beneath that exterior — a heart which, unfortunately, gave way several years ago. At any rate, when Himber trapped you in his lair and tried to foist some of his new magical brainchildren on you, it took a lot of willpower to fight him off. Most of the time I succeeded, for a very simple reason. I couldn't afford them. But, as I said, I did acquire a few, some of which have become collectors' items.

Another magical enthusiast I met in New York was Ed Mishell. Ed, a successful lawyer, was a living example of the term "magical enthusiast." I often wondered when he found time to look after his law career. Whenever I visited Tannen's, Mishell was there. Whatever group I gathered with, there he was again. He was also an artist, and did all the artwork for Tannen's huge magic catalog for years, in addition to drawing sketches for various magic magazines. And I have a hunch he did not push for monetary gain in these activities — he enjoyed doing them so much.

At his home in New Jersey he set up a magic den that was a showplace, with a built-in stage and all the accoutrements that go with it, and a lavish display of magical paraphernalia. Ed was also an avid antique collector. Whereas Himber would entice me to his apartment, Mishell would drag me from one antique shop to another to keep him company while he searched for yet another prized possession.

For many years, any magician visiting New York would do his utmost to drop in to the Hotel Dixie dining room on 42nd Street in the Times Square area, at lunchtime. It was there that magicians held forth around the Dixie Magic Table — actually a group of tables that some New York magicians arranged to have set aside every lunch hour at this busy restaurant. The place became a mecca for local and visiting conjurers. You would always find a number of top-flight performers on hand, and the fun was fast and furious. One magician would always try to top another with a new effect. We also had lunch, of course, but I cannot recall anything I was served, let alone what I ordered — and I never finished a meal. Since then, the Magic Table has moved to other establishments, but I believe it still exists.

Another major magic shop I used to visit in Manhattan was that of Al Flosso, the Coney Island Fakir — whom we'll meet again in a later chapter. Al's shop, called the Hornmann Magic Company, was probably the oldest operating magic emporium in the world, with a history going back to 1856. It was located on 34th Street, not far from the Empire State Building. At the turn of the century it was the famous Martinka Magic Shop, where the Society of American Magicians was founded in 1902. The shop was purchased in 1919 by Harry Houdini, who ran it for a brief time. Al Flosso took over the business in 1938 and maintained it until his death in 1976.

To get to the shop you would enter a bar, mount a set of dingy steps to the second floor, and enter a scene of magical confusion. Where Tannen's was a modern shop with glittering showcases and wallcases and everything neat and tidy, Flosso's was full of foggy glass showcases littered with all sorts of magical articles — undusted, of course. Some looked as if they hadn't been moved for years. The light fixtures and wallcases were Victorian. But the real goodies and magic collectors' items, many from another age, were stocked in the famous "back room."

In the old days every magic shop had its back room. Potential customers could not just wander in from the street and purchase any item. Since the secrets of magic were guarded more carefully then than they are today, the would-be purchaser would usually be interviewed and questioned about his magical capacities before being admitted to the back room, where the deal would be consummated. Today, you can just walk in, make your purchase, and you are an instant magician. At least, you'll think you are.

Al Flosso, a short man, well along in years, was a typically abrasive, but good-natured New Yorker. He had all the manner-isms of a carnival barker. When I'd come through the doorway he would always greet me with, "Hello, m'boy, how ya doin'?" Many a pleasurable hour I spent with Al and with the various assorted characters who would drop in to his shop from time to time. He had been a friend of Houdini and many other magical greats, and was a veritable storehouse of magical lore. While customers puttered around the shop he would ignore them, sitting and talking with me about magic and magicians, past and present. He did have great patience and was very helpful when youngsters, starting out in magic, came in for tricks and advice.

Whenever I asked Flosso to suggest a trick I might purchase, he would say, "Just a second, I've got something you've never seen," and disappear into the back room — then emerge with a contrap-tion that could have been constructed during the American Civil War. Caressing it lovingly, he would demonstrate it for me, and then, if I expressed an interest in buying it, he would say, "Nah, I've had this a long time. I don't think I'll let it go."

I watched with amusement as he pulled this caper with many a customer. He really was sincere. He was so attached to many of his props that he really did prefer to keep them than make a profitable sale. I once talked him into selling me a small item that he had first decided to retain, and my conscience bothered me for weeks afterward.

A regular visitor at Flosso's was a man I had heard on radio and read about for years — Joseph Dunninger, the renowned mentalist.

Another close acquaintance of Houdini, he branched out from performing straight magic into the mind-reading field, and became the greatest act of that kind in the business. He was the first to present his mental miracles on network radio and then on television. Some of the tips I got from Joe Dunninger were priceless, particularly when mentalism became my specialty. One of today's most successful mind-reading performers based his act entirely on Dunninger's presentation, but he will never approach the master in technique and authority.

While attending meetings of the Society of American Magicians in New York I discovered how many superb amateur magicians were drawn to the hobby from many walks of life. I've already mentioned Ed Mishell, but there were several other prominent New York lawyers on the scene. Then there was Dr. Jacob Daley, a leading plastic surgeon at French Hospital. Dr. Daley sometimes took time out from his busy practice to perform at business and corporate functions. His technique in sleight-of-hand was superior to that of many professionals. He was considered a leader in the field.

Max Katz, owner of a large jewelry firm, was another skilful and dedicated amateur. Max's great intellect was put to good use by the U.S. government in World War II when he was employed as a cipher agent in Washington. He turned that intellect to good use after the war when he became immersed in the development and presentation of magical effects.

Another interesting gentleman I met in New York during that period was the well-known author William Gresham, whose popular novel *Nightmare Alley* was made into a movie starring the late Tyrone Power. Bill Gresham always had an interest in magicians and circus sideshow characters, and loved to write about them. I remember walking down Broadway with him one day while he was researching the book *Houdini*, which turned out to be one of the best of the Houdini biographies. He regaled me with anecdotes about the legendary escape artist, some of which appear further along in this book. Bill Gresham later died a tragic death, a suicide.

New York City, being the metropolis it is, has probably always been a world capital of Magic. I had the good fortune to visit the city frequently at a time when contemporary figures who had a linkup with past great artists were still around. The new generation

Rope magic by the Gordons on a cruise ship in the 1960s.

of magicians is probably more technically clever and advanced than the old one, but it seems to me that some of the color, some of the romance of conjuring has disappeared. Who knows? We all like to talk about the "good old days," don't we? Time moves on, and the scene changes.

My New York connections led to a series of bookings on cruise ships in the 1960s and 1970s. There really is no better way to spend a vacation. Zita (my stage assistant on these cruises) and I would be assigned a comfortable cabin and all the amenities available to the average passenger — at no cost. I considered my salary a bonus. For all this we performed our act a mere two nights a week.

We worked for Greek Lines and Holland America Lines.

Holland America's flagship, SS *Rotterdam*, was by far the most luxurious ship we sailed on. The staff actually included a professional magician, who went on every cruise. He performed mainly large stage illusions, and was assigned a special cabin packed with these props. My act was an added attraction on this ship.

All the cruises embarked from New York, and sailed to various ports in the Caribbean and to Nassau and Bermuda. There was only one problem with sailing out of New York. When we passed Cape Hatteras, things could get a little rough, with choppy seas and the odd storm. The good cruise life would carry on — but on a tilt.

It was around that area, when we were on the *Ryndam*, one of Holland America's smaller ships, that we ran into a whopping big storm one evening. And it was a night when we had a show coming up. Dinner was not a resounding success: half the dining tables were unoccupied. The evening cabaret show was scheduled to begin right after dinner.

The opening act was to be a dance team, followed by our magic act. While we were setting up in the backstage dressing room an agitated cruise director burst in, "You're on." "Where's the dance team?" I asked. "Sick. Let's go." "You OK, Zita?" I asked. The answer was a weak "I think so."

Standing on the tilting stage, I sized up the situation. The orchestra seemed to be playing normally enough — as normally as they ever played after spending most of the day in one of the bars. The audience was a little sparse — understandable. Some of them looked as if they might not be around to see the conclusion of my performance. Oh well, as they say, the show must go on.

It went fairly well, with the odd interruption, when I had to hiss out of the side of my mouth, "Zita, grab the table!" You see, I was using what we call a roll-on table, a small unit mounted on casters, which held my props. Zita would stand beside it, handing me props and receiving them after I had performed the effect — in the time-honored magic assistant's manner. The problem was that every time the ship pitched and tossed, the table would start rolling off the stage.

Meanwhile, every now and then, a couple would get up and depart. The audience was really beginning to thin out. I wasn't sure if it was the storm or the act. I couldn't care less, because by then I was beginning to feel a bit queasy myself.

Finally, and mercifully, we came to the big finale, the climax of my act — the light-bulb trick. The illusion was this: Zita would hand me a length of thin wire. I would roll it up into a small ball and swallow it. She would then hand me a small stand on which half a dozen lit-up flashlight bulbs were fastened. I would hold the stand and pick off one bulb at a time, with my teeth. I would swallow each one in turn. As I handed the stand back to Zita, the stage lights would dim, the drummer would start a long, dramatic drum roll, I would reach my thumb and forefinger into my mouth — and pull out the length of wire, with the six bulbs strung out on it at regular intervals, each one still lit. A great closing effect, which always drew heavy applause.

As we were proceeding with the routine, two things preyed on my mind. First, this was a heck of a night to perform a regurgitation trick. Second, would we lose the table? I did not foresee the other possibility, which actually did happen. I lost my assistant!

When I handed the small light stand to Zita after I had swallowed the bulbs, she wasn't there. Neither was the table. A complete vanishing act — and it wasn't even part of our program.

Somehow I maintained my composure, completed the effect, and ran off to a smattering of applause. Back in the dressing room I found my assistant leaning on the table, green-faced, but recovering. Sheer willpower had kept her on stage through most of the act, but in those final moments good sense won out. At least she'd had the presence of mind to take the roving table with her.

In 1986, when Zita and I were attending a convention in Boulder, Colorado, we decided to take a side trip to California and explore the Los Angeles and San Diego areas. There was one place in Los Angeles we had always wanted to visit — the famous Hollywood Magic Castle. So I called Bill Larsen, who owns and runs it, to let him know we would be dropping in. Our conversation ended with Bill inviting me to deliver a lecture while we were there. This visit proved to be a highlight of our trip.

If you feel comfortable talking to an owl or conversing with a piano, you'll be right at home visiting the Hollywood Magic Castle.

This famous magical showplace is perched on a hillside on

Franklin Avenue in the center of Hollywood, just north of the landmark Chinese Theatre. Surrounded by palms, the turreted structure dominates the area. It is actually a Gothic Victorian mansion originally built in 1908 and restored by the Castle's creator, Milt Larsen.

After you drive up the steep, beautifully landscaped driveway and reach the grand fountain with its spouting lions, you come to an ornate entrance with a façade of stained glass and cut crystal. You enter the building and find yourself in a small reception hall with book-lined shelves. There is no apparent exit from this room other than the doorway through which you have just entered. The receptionist at the desk verifies your entrance credentials, and then, if you're a first-time visitor, you will usually ask where you go from there. You will be directed, "Just turn around and say 'Open Sesame' to the owl."

Feeling rather self-conscious, you turn and find yourself facing a bronze owl with mysteriously blinking eyes. Only by addressing the owl with the magical words "Open Sesame" will you gain admittance to the inner sanctum. A secret door swings open and you enter the dining and showplace areas.

Once inside, you find yourself in a veritable wonderland of magic. There are several theater areas: the Close-up Gallery is an intimate room with tiered seating, enabling a good view of a magician performing card and coin miracles on a tabletop; the Parlour of Prestidigitation is a larger room, seating sixty-five spectators and designed for stand-up magic that does not require a large stage area; the Palace of Mystery is a fully equipped theatre — small, but with a good-sized stage and superb lighting and sound system.

These show rooms each feature several acts nightly, with a change of performers each week. And these performers comprise some of the cream of the magical world. An appearance at the Magic Castle carries a lot of prestige. Once or twice a month knowledgeable magicians deliver lectures at the Castle for those who have a more technical interest in the art.

But aside from the Castle's magical entertainment, the various "magical museum" rooms are a popular attraction. The Robert-Houdin Museum room has an intriguing display of nineteenth-century magical apparatus — collector's items from another era.

Robert-Houdin, known as the Father of Modern Magic, was the great French illusionist from whom Harry Houdini borrowed his name. Other rooms, their walls lined with pictures and posters, are dedicated to such past magical greats as Dante and Harry Blackstone, Sr.

One of the main attractions is the Houdini Seance Room. Surrounded by some of Houdini's original artifacts and by memorabilia of his fabulous career is a large, round dining table, set with fine silver and crystal stemware. Dinner reservations, booked months ahead, can be made for parties of twelve only. A thirteenth chair remains unoccupied.

After a gourmet dinner, a "medium" enters the room and occupies the vacant chair — after which the seance begins and strange phenomena start to occur. All the effects, of course, are manipulations of the magician's art. Houdini himself spent the last years of his life debunking and exposing the spirit mediums of his day.

The Houdini Seance Room may be one of the most elaborate features of the Magic Castle, but the most widely discussed phenomenon is probably Invisible Irma. Irma was one of the seven sisters who were supposed to have inhabited the building at the turn of the century. She was the only one who was musically inclined, and practised the piano daily. The constant playing was so irritating to the family that she and her piano were banished to a small room in the tower.

This so embittered Irma that before she died, in 1932, she vowed she would return to haunt the house. And she has. Her ghost performs daily in the Music Chamber. There her grand piano stands — and not only does she play it, but she will play almost any tune a visitor requests. Her repertoire is truly uncanny, as is the appearance of the keys being depressed as Irma's invisible fingers skim over them. Place a glass with a beverage on the piano and you will see the contents visibly diminish as Irma imbibes. The entire presentation is spooky, entertaining — and memorable.

The story behind the establishment of the Magic Castle is almost as intriguing as the Castle itself. William W. Larsen, Sr. was a noted criminal lawyer in Los Angeles. He was also a dedicated magician and the original publisher of *Genii: The Conjurer's Magazine*, a monthly periodical which is still distributed around the world.

In 1953 he founded the Academy of Magical Arts and Sciences, a magical society, with the eventual goal of establishing a clubhouse along the lines of the Magic Circle in London, England. When William Larsen, Sr. died in 1956, his son, Bill, Jr., took over and still runs the magazine. He and his brother Milt never forgot their father's dream. In 1962, when the opportunity arose to get possession of the Castle property, the brothers acted.

Even though they were fully occupied with television careers — Milt wrote for some major network productions, while Bill helped produce the old *Danny Kaye Show* — they devoted a good part of their energies to the new project. Milt, particularly, worked long hours, doing physical labour to help renovate the structure and give it its present appearance.

The Magic Castle is headquarters for a private club, which now includes over five thousand members, including two thousand magicians. The late actor Cary Grant, a longtime magic buff, was one of the club's directors, along with some of the great names on the contemporary magic scene.

Even though the Castle is a private club, the public is not excluded. One need only be accompanied by a member or a visiting magician or carry a note from an accredited magician to be admitted. The Hollywood Magic Castle is a must for anyone visiting the Los Angeles area.

Would you believe that being a magician led me to deliver lectures on witchcraft in Salem, Massachusetts the witchcraft capital of the United States? When Dr. Donald Burke of John Proctor Productions called, back in 1983, he made me an offer I couldn't refuse. "Could you come down here to Salem this summer? I'd like you to produce and appear in a stage show including a performance of magic and a lecture on the subject of witchcraft. We have a comfortable house on the bay for you and your wife, and we'd be glad to put a car at your disposal."

The offer was to lead to one of my most interesting experiences. Salem, Massachusetts, known as "Witch City," is a town unlike most others. It is the third-oldest settlement on the continent and was one of the principal ports in early America. It was also the location of the notorious witch craze of 1692, so graphically portrayed in Arthur Miller's play, *The Crucible*. This sad story of witchcraft hysteria and its subsequent trials is now the main tourist attraction for this town of forty thousand souls.

Walk through its business district and you will notice that the majority of outdoor signs on storefronts and on many institutions feature the word "witch." The Salem Chamber of Commerce, of course, encourage this. Witchcraft is what makes Salem one of the top tourist destinations in the United States.

One of the town's leading citizens is Laurie Cabot, the official witch of Salem. She is a busy lady. Her downtown shop is a thriving dispensary of all manner of occult books, exotic herbs, and witchcraft artifacts. In 1983 she was head of a coven of witches, mostly young people, numbering over four hundred. In 1983 she was broadcasting a brief, daily witchcraft report on a Boston radio station, and teaching a regular witchcraft course in nearby Marblehead. In 1988, according to newspaper reports, she actually ran for the office of mayor of Salem.

Another colorful character we met was Bruce Michaud who owned the famous Salem Witch Museum, the town's leading tourist attraction. We noticed that buses were continually unloading tourists at the door. Bruce also owned the bus company. A charming, friendly man who loved magic, he gave us a grand tour of the town in his new Rolls-Royce, pointing out its many historical highlights. He also showed us the town's large new-car dealership — which he also owned.

I managed to put together a rather interesting presentation at the Salem Theater. We called it *The Witchcraft Secrets*. John Proctor Productions did a good job of advertising, including putting up colorful posters all over town. Strangely, these posters would always disappear by the next morning. It seems that certain citizens resented the appearance in their midst of a magician with skeptical leanings about the paranormal.

I was asked to return in the fall to take part in Salem's annual Hallowe'en bash, Haunted Happenings. On this occasion my presentation at the theater was called *The Houdini Secrets*, in which I did some conjuring, including a few escapes, and a talk about the immortal escape artist who died on Hallowe'en. The town holds a whole series of spooky events on this occasion, including a giant parade — and the tourists flock in. Witchcraft works — at least financially.

II
Magicians Past and Present

5
The History of Magic

In a general sense, this book is about magic. But it would be more accurate to say that it is about conjuring. The difference? Magic is defined as an occult art by which nature or natural events are controlled or influenced by supernatural means. Conjuring, or legerdemain, or prestidigitation, is the accomplishment of the apparently supernatural by natural means. When we speak of a magician today, we are speaking of an actor playing the part of a magician. The modern magician is a performer who asks you to sit back, suspend your disbelief, and for a few minutes or a few hours, enter into a fantasy world of make-believe.

Magic has always been a universal performing art. It began back in antiquity, and was probably first used by the ancient priests to impress and control the masses. It consisted mostly of chants, rituals and magic spells. Strangely, however, all this mumbo jumbo actually had a part in building the foundations of modern science. Magic and science have progressed side by side down through the centuries.

Alchemy was an art that bridged the gap between the two domains. According to occultists, the alchemists' goal was to unlock the secrets of the formation of matter. Although alchemists may have discovered some of these secrets along the way, it is more likely that their main goal was to discover how to make artificial gold. In any case, the alchemists and the potion mixers and the herb gatherers were precursors of the pharmacists and chemists we know today. Star-gazing prophets developed the concept of astrology, which finally transformed itself into the

51

science of astronomy — with astrology still hanging on tenaciously.

The Babylonians originally used the positions of the stars and planets for practical reasons — in order to predict the times of floods for irrigational purposes. Astrology grew out of this, then finally became the science of astronomy as it is known today.

People have always wanted to look into the future. Hence, the development of astrology and divination of all kinds, such as reading the shape of the face, the lines of the face, the shape of the head, the lines of the hands, the entrails of animals, Tarot cards, the crystal ball. The modern mentalist-magician has taken a cue from all these devices to develop the so-called mind-reading act, which exerts a stronger influence on many people than does the performing of illusions.

The reason for this is simple enough — most people realize that the woman floating in space is suspended by some sort of mechanical, if hidden, contrivance. But when the performer reveals some supposedly secret piece of information which they *think* he or she could not possibly know by natural means, a profound impression is often made. The mentalist, of course, has many means by which he can secretly secure information. It's part of the act, and the honest stage performer doesn't try to mask that fact. That is the big difference between the conjurer and the fraudulent "psychic."

What is thought to be the first recorded conjuring performance for a monarch was described in a hieroglyphic inscription thousands of years ago. The monarch was Cheops, builder of the Great Pyramid in Egypt, and the performance described took place in 2700 BC. The conjurer's name was Dedi.

The earliest known record of an actual magic trick is a drawing of the Cups and Balls effect found on the wall of a burial chamber in Egypt. This drawing is estimated to have been made in about 2500 BC. It is amazing to consider that this trick has survived eons and is still a popular conjuring effect today. This is probably because the Cups and Balls effect encompasses most of the basic effects of magic. Objects appear, disappear, multiply, change color, change their locations, and penetrate solids. And the only artifacts you need are three solid cups and a few small balls.

Actually, balls are not always used. Some years ago I was fortunate enough to witness the act of a fantastic Egyptian wizard named Galli Galli. He would show three inverted cups to be empty, then produce a baby chick under each one. He'd go on to a bewildering routine, in which the chirping chicks would materialize, dematerialize, change places, then multiply until he had dozens of tiny chicks hopping around the table. His nightclub act always brought down the house.

The history of conjuring through the centuries is an interesting one, but it is not my intention to describe its full historical development. That subject has been covered well by several authors already. I would prefer to update this narrative by bringing us into the modern era of magic, which got its real start in the nineteenth century.

During that era the stage magician was a leader in the world of entertainment. His feats were looked upon with awe. He commanded attention with some pretty grisly effects, such as burning people alive and then having them materialize from the ashes. The Talking Head was popular too: the magician would appear to slice off somebody's head and place it on a table, then the eyes would open and the head would begin speaking.

Even in the nineteenth century magicians were using new technology. And since then magicians have continued to use new technical developments to perform their miracles before most members of the public were even aware they existed. The great French conjurer, Robert-Houdin, used electromagnetism to accomplish one of his most celebrated effects when the phenomenon was still unknown to most. I will describe this effect in the following chapter.

Magicians today use many of the wonders of science and technology now at their disposal: electronics, magnetism, fiber optics, and anything else that is available. However, modern magicians face one problem that their nineteenth-century counterparts did not have to face. Today's public is much more sophisticated and difficult to impress. The illusion may work, but the audience will take it with a grain of salt. Right or wrong, the viewers will often attribute the effect to some easily accepted miracle of science, rather than to the cleverness or skill of the magician.

That, I believe, is one of the main reasons why many magical illusions on television leave audiences cold. When a performer magically floats across the Grand Canyon and the viewers are informed there are no camera tricks involved, any rational person will still infer that there is *some* ultra-technical hanky panky taking place. Somehow it doesn't have the same impact as the floating lady seen live onstage. For myself, it doesn't even have as much impact as a well-executed card trick.

But, getting back to the 1800s, near the end of the century magical performers began using a radical new technology: the cinema. The idea of projecting images was not a new one to the world of magic; the novelty of cinema was that its images could move. In fact, magicians had already been using slide projectors (called "magic lanterns") for more than a century when moving pictures first came on the scene.

A Belgian who used the name of Robertson was among the first to use the magic lantern, in a startling performance called *Fantasmagorie*, which he first exhibited in Paris. He would toss some chemicals on hot coals, causing smoke to rise, then project all sorts of spooky images upon the smoke. He devised a system of rear projection, so that the audience had no idea where the apparitions were coming from. The images themselves were fashioned through prepared glass slides fastened to the front of the lantern. Robertson's show was a sensation. Other magicians soon borrowed the idea to help create new illusions in their presentations.

When moving pictures were being developed, many magic artists saw their "magical" potential long before films became a popular entertainment. They began to perform in front of the cameras, then included their film performances as part of their stage presentations. But this posed a problem: their film feats so dwarfed their stage tricks that they eventually put themselves out of business. The reason for this? They were using trick photography, which produced apparent miracles that could never be matched on stage. Ironically, magicians were responsible for the early development and popularity of "movies," which, in turn, hastened the decline in popularity of their own art.

Still, in the early part of the twentieth century, magic maintained a fairly high profile in the entertainment world — perhaps not as high in America as in Britain and on the European continent. The full-evening theater show was in great favor, and magicians appeared on almost every vaudeville bill. The huge touring stage shows of such magical greats as Kellar, Dante, Carter, Nicola, Herrmann, Thurston, Blackstone, and many others, played to packed houses. Great sleight-of-hand performers like Downs, Leipzig, Fowler, and Cardini, were the stars of any program in which they appeared.

And, of course, the immortal Harry Houdini caught the public imagination more than any other magician, before or since. His sensational escapes from any form of confinement and his unmatched ability to squeeze every bit of publicity out of his feats kept the art of magic front and center for years.

Houdini was one of the first to switch from presenting a potpourri of magic tricks to specializing in one particular type of effect — in his case the challenge escape. The 1930s marked the beginning of the age of the specialists, particularly among those who performed in clubs or vaudeville.

The mentalist, or mind-reading, act also gained great popularity. Then came the cigarette specialist. For years, any magician worth his salt learned to pull lighted cigarettes out of the air, and manipulate them, making them vanish and reappear. Indeed, that was one of my own specialties for a while. I went even further, doing the act with lighted pipes! On today's social scene, however, an act like this would definitely lay an egg.

The card specialist had his day, too pulling not cigarettes but playing cards out of the air. Then there were the great coin manipulators who did nothing but conjuring with coins. This act is still popular among close-up magicians, but in earlier days it was presented as a stage act. Dove magic came along in the post-war period, and it is still popular — although I feel the public has now had a surfeit of this type of presentation. Producing live doves out of nothingness *is* a showy stunt, and magic with any kind of livestock has always been popular, particularly with the junior set. But it seems that in recent years the symbolic magician's rabbit has been replaced by the fluttering dove. A pity.

Have you ever wondered why the rabbit and the dove are so popular with magicians? Without giving away too many trade secrets, I will explain. These two little creatures are small and quiet — and so will not reveal their places of concealment. Places of concealment? Have I shattered any illusions about real magic?

As the years went by and vaudeville began to die out, the

nightclubs took up some of the slack. But then the touring theater shows began to run into trouble. The high costs of traveling and of staging ornate magical extravaganzas started to take their toll. The big-name shows began dropping off one by one, and as nightclubs began to close, the professional magis entered a very lean period. Television provided some work, but hardly enough. This is still the situation today on the professional magic scene.

But what has changed tremendously is the rise of magic as a hobby, a diversion, as an amateur and semi-professional occcupation by thousands of members of the general public. This transformation has occurred as a result of the lifting of the veil of secrecy that has always surrounded the art. Oldtime conjurers jealously guarded their secrets from all but the privileged few. Then, eventually, the odd book was published, revealing some of the magical methods. With the formation of magic societies and the publication of magic magazines, even more information became available to those who took a particular interest in the subject.

It is interesting to note that until about the 1960s magic books were available only at established magic shops. The general reading public was never exposed to these books in regular bookstores. You would not even be holding the book you are now reading unless you were a magic shop customer. First of all, this type of book would be published only by companies that specialized in producing books on conjuring. But as public interest in the art began to grow, non-specialty publishers took notice and began to realize that there was a market out there.

Many in the magic field still resent this exposure of magic secrets to the public. The controversy has been raging among magicians for many years. Should we tell all about magic or should we keep our knowledge to ourselves?

Let's set this scenario: you are relaxing, reading a book by one of your favorite whodunit authors. The plot is getting more complicated. You can't wait to get to the big scene where the super detective reveals all to the gathered suspects. A friend walks in, sees what you are reading, and exclaims, "Great book, well written," and proceeds to tell you how the whole thing winds up. Not only that, he spots two other mystery books on the side table, waiting for your consumption — and gleefully describes their plots and how the mysteries are solved.

What would your reaction be? "Thanks, saves me the time and the enjoyment of reading these books," or would your response perhaps be on the violent side? You can compare this to having the secret of a magic trick exposed in advance. Spoils your fun.

So where should we draw the line when it comes to magical exposure? My opinion is that if someone is interested enough to spend money to buy a magic book or take a magic course, there is nothing wrong with accommodating that person. On the other hand, it is not really ethical to reveal magical methods gratis, just for the sake of satisfying someone's curiosity. That kind of offhand revelation should be discouraged. Countless times media people have tried to pry secrets out of me to be revealed in turn to their readers, listeners, and viewers — with varying promises of media publicity for myself. I have devised equally countless ways of saying "Thanks, but no thanks."

There are more ways than one of enjoying the hobby of magic. I know many magic devotees who have never performed a trick in their lives. One gentleman, who must go unnamed, has invented some of the most ingenious effects in card magic, but literally quakes if he is asked to demonstrate one of his own tricks. To him, it is satisfying enough simply to devise effects. He is one of a small but elite breed who specialize in invention.

There are many who do not "magish" but who have a vast knowledge of the subject. Other non-performers are collectors who accumulate masses of magical apparatus and magic books. The ranks of the collectors, of course, also include many performing magicians. Rabid collectors of books on conjuring will travel to all parts of the world to add to their stock, if they can afford it. Some will collect posters advertising great magic acts of the past or any sort of material used by famous magicians.

Lucky is the person who can find the time and the dollars to indulge in all the aspects of this wonderful art. To invent magical effects is a challenge to the intellect and to one's reasoning powers. To join the ranks of the collectors is to belong to a worldwide group of interesting people with a common cause, and to learn the colorful history of the ancient art.

But to actually perform, to be a magician — that is the icing on the cake. Remember, I am referring here to the amateur magician. What other activity will provide these benefits? You will develop

57

The lightbulb production

your motor skills; you will learn much about psychology and its uses; you will develop confidence in yourself; you will get the satisfaction of being able to entertain others, and to bring a smile to the faces of the ill and the disabled.

And what about the practical benefits to the salesperson, the businessperson, or to anyone else who comes in contact with the public? It is amazing how the presentation of a well-conceived magic illusion pulled from your pocket will open doors and establish friendly relations. This has been proven over and over again.

You may gather from all this that I am rather enthusiastic about the art of magic. I am!

Magic has undergone many transformations since it appeared in Cheops's Egyptian court, but even in our sophisticated times, people are drawn — often in spite of themselves — to the ancient art.

6
Great Magicians of the Past

When I decided to write about the lives and careers of some of the eminent conjurers of other ages I encountered a problem, a problem of choices. There are so many from which to choose. To cover all the important magicians of history, one would have to devote an entire book to the subject. In this chapter, I have concentrated on the few whom I felt had the greatest impact on the magical scene in general, and those whose careers I personally found most intriguing.

In the early part of the nineteenth century, Jean-Eugene Robert, son of a French watchmaker, learned that craft himself and practised it for years in his birthplace, Blois. He later turned his mechanical abilities to the making of automata, the mechanical toys that were so popular at the time. Although he showed an early interest in conjuring, he wasn't really serious about it for years, confining himself mostly to card trickery. Later, when he joined an amateur theatrical company in Blois, he made his first stage appearances — but as an actor, not a magician. It was his association with the theater, however, that led him to concoct a name that was to become famous in the world of magic. After he was married, he added his wife's surname, Houdin, to his own and created his immortal stage-name: Jean Robert-Houdin. Under this moniker he became known as the Father of Modern Magic.

Meanwhile, he was becoming celebrated for the apparently magical contrivances he was constructing. One of these, the magical clock, had a glass dial standing on a glass pillar, all completely transparent — yet the hands on the dial would move, keeping perfect time. The secret? The minute and hour markings were inscribed on a stationary section of the dial. A second glass portion of the dial revolved in front of the stationary one, moving the hands between them. The movement was invisible because it was glass moving over glass.

But what made the dial turn? The glass pillar on which the dial rested was hollowed out. Inside it was a glass rod that was geared to the rim of the movable dial. The bottom of the rod was connected to a mechanism hidden inside the stand that supported the pillar. Again, the rotation of the rod could not be seen because it was glass moving inside glass — all transparent. Robert-Houdin was probably the first to use the principle of the transparency of glass to create magical effects.

A far simpler adaptation of this principle is used to this day. Have you ever seen the eye-catching display of a faucet suspended in air by a wire, water streaming out of it endlessly, into a container down below? And have you wondered where the water was coming from? A glass rod inserted in the mouth of the faucet extends down to the water container below, where a small pump forces the liquid back up to the top of the rod. The water then spills back down from the mouth of the faucet, and so the cycle continues. The glass rod is inside the stream of water, and since it is transparent, it cannot be seen.

Robert-Houdin was well into his middle years before he began to make his mark as a stage magician. Inspired by some of the performers he saw after he moved to Paris, he began to plan a show of his own. His mechanical abilities allowed him to construct some ingenious and completely original apparatus. He was also among those who took advantage of the newest technological developments to create illusions.

His presentation of the Light and Heavy Chest became a sensation. He put a small wooden box on the stage. Then he'd ask any husky grown man from the audience to come on stage and lift up the box. One after another would come up and struggle and heave, but the box would not budge. Then the magician would invite a small boy to come up. The youngster would pick up the box effortlessly. The audience — with the possible exception of the humiliated strongmen — found the whole thing most amusing, yet there seemed to be no explanation for it. Here Robert-Houdin used the principle of electromagnetism, of which very few were aware. A powerful electromagnet was fastened under the stage covering on which the box rested. Wires from the electromagnet ran to a backstage location, where an assistant controlled a switch. The box itself had an iron plate in the bottom. When the electromagnet was switched on, the magnetic attraction between the iron plate and the magnet made it impossible to lift the box. When the child came onstage, the assistant flipped the switch and cut off the current.

Robert-Houdin was also the first to succeed in making a person appear suspended in midair. He used his son as the subject. The boy would stand on a stool, an upright rod set in a platform on each side of him. He would rest an elbow on each rod. The magician would remove the stool, and the boy would remain suspended on his elbows. Robert-Houdin would then move one of his son's arms so that it was hanging at his side and he was now resting on one elbow only. He then lifted the boy's body to a horizontal position, where he remained suspended, just resting on one vertical rod with his elbow. The spectators began rubbing their eyes in disbelief.

This illusion has remained popular to this day, so the method used to achieve it cannot be revealed. It is now known as the Broomstick Illusion, with the suspended subject resting an armpit over the business end of a broomstick. Some magicians use a sword as the vertical support, just for variety.

Robert-Houdin's presentation of this effect is just another example of how this supreme showman modernized magical presentation and made use of up-to-date developments. At that time the new anesthetic, ether, had just been discovered. Now, when you see a magician suspend a lady in the air you will usually see him first "hypnotize" her, appearing to render her unconscious. Robert-Houdin instead passed a small opened bottle, ostensibly containing ether, under his son's nose before suspending him. The boy would then seem to be rendered insensible.

This had a strong psychological effect on the audience because they were already deeply impressed by the "magical" effects of this new anesthetic. To add to the effect, the odor of ether was wafted throughout the auditorium. Of course it didn't emanate from the bottle, which was what the audience believed. The bottle was empty. But an assistant backstage was busy pouring ether on a heated pan — which only proves that magicians will go to any lengths to accomplish their miracles.

In 1856 Jean Robert-Houdin accomplished his greatest magic feat. He was summoned to Algiers by the French government to help put down a potential revolt by some Algerian tribesmen. The Marabouts, local wonder-workers, were using their own conjurings to egg on their tribesmen. The French authorities decided that the rebellion might be averted if a French magician could impress the Arab leaders by outperforming the Marabouts.

Robert-Houdin set up a full stage show in a theater, and the Arab leaders were invited. It's doubtful that they had even sat in a theater before. When he began producing things from nowhere and presenting the various standard magical tricks of the trade, they were visibly thunderstruck. When he presented the Light and Heavy Chest illusion he did not do his usual humorous presentation. Instead, he announced through an interpreter that he would turn the strongest man in the house into a powerless weakling. The first volunteer swaggered up onto the stage. The magician asked him to lift the chest. The man grabbed the two handles and lifted the chest high in the air, then replaced it disdainfully. Robert-Houdin then announced that he had now deprived the man of his strength and challenged him to lift it again. Again he grasped the handles and pulled. He began to struggle when he found the box wouldn't budge. Suddenly he began to writhe and groan. When he finally let go, he ran screaming out of the theater.

Robert-Houdin had added a little touch to the presentation. In addition to having the electromagnet energized, he had put a little extra wiring on the handles that would send out a small electric shock when he gave the signal to the stagehand in the wings.

His performance was a sensational success. The tribesmen had never seen anything like it. The great magician had accomplished his mission.

As a stage magician, Robert-Houdin set the standard for all the magicians who followed in the modern era. He brought an actor's skill to the performance of magic. And we all remember his famous quotation, "A magician is an actor playing the part of a magician."

He died at his home, Saint-Gervais, on June 13, 1871, at the age of sixty-five.

It was the evening of March 23, 1918. The audience at the Wood Green Empire Theatre in London, England, was enjoying a superb magic show. During a pause in the program, a steady drumroll was heard coming from the orchestra pit. At one side of the stage two uniformed men carrying muskets took their positions, raised the firearms to their shoulders, and took aim. At the other side, directly in the line of fire, stood an elaborately robed Chinese magician, the star of the show. He held a china plate in front of his chest.

The muskets roared. The magician dropped to the floor, bleeding heavily. Illusion had turned to tragedy. It was the end for the world-famous magician, Chung Ling Soo, probably the greatest of the Chinese conjurers.

Only he wasn't Chinese. His real name was William Ellsworth Robinson, and he was born in New York City of parents of Scottish descent.

Bill Robinson began his professional magic career as the "Man of Mystery," touring New England with his act while still a teenager. He performed all the standard tricks of the day and was moderately successful. But he was smart enough to realize that he would have to come up with something special to really stand out. One day he saw a performer present "Black Art" and immediately decided that was it.

In Black Art, the entire stage is covered with black velvet — the floor, the ceiling, the side and rear walls. The front lighting (in Robinson's time it was provided by gas burners) is directed mostly toward the audience to help make the blackness of the stage really solid. Anything onstage that is covered with or hidden by black velvet material will be invisible to the audience. For instance, a person dressed totally in black and wearing a black hood and black gloves will not be seen; only white objects are visible.

Just think of one small possibility. The performer can pull a white handkerchief out of his pocket, toss it into the air, catch it and replace it in his pocket. What the audience sees is a handkerchief materializing out of nowhere, flying in the air, then disappearing. The effect is uncanny.

Many elaborate and entertaining Black Art acts have been

presented over the years. Robinson's was one of them. He was a huge success on the vaudeville circuits.

In 1899 an unknown new wizard, Ching Ling Foo, arrived in America from China. It was he who started the trend toward Chinese-style magic in the West. This type of magic act blended elaborate costuming with exotic effects — tricks not seen before on European or American stages.

Ching's most astounding feat was the production of a giant-sized porcelain bowl filled with gallons of water, on an empty stage. He would simply walk out on stage slowly, wave a huge silk cloth in front of him, pull it aside, and reveal a huge bowl of water sitting there — eighteen inches high and of the same diameter. And a dozen apples would be floating in the water.

Only a magician garbed in a Chinese-style floor-length loose robe could have accomplished this feat. The bowl was suspended under his robe and behind his legs by a special harness fitted with a self-releasing hook. As Ching waved the silk cloth in front of him he would crouch slightly. The bowl would touch the floor, the hook would release, he would step back, whip away the cloth and voilà, the bowl of water!

Ching's act was so commercially successful that he spawned several imitators. William Robinson was the most successful of these. As a matter of fact, Chung Ling Soo, the imitator, became far more successful than Ching Ling Foo, the original. Robinson's Chinese makeup was masterly, and he was accepted as an Oriental wherever he appeared professionally.

Robinson was also one of the first to perform the Aerial Fishing illusion. Visualize the magician standing at the edge of the stage holding a long pole. He throws a line out above the audience and begins pulling fish out of the air, tossing each one into a fishbowl.

And here's one you don't see performed today. Chung would have his female assistant stand at centerstage. He would fire an arrow, with a string attached, right through the poor girl into a target behind her. And there was the string penetrating her body. Shades of William Tell. This type of effect, the guillotine effect, and cutting a woman in half are what I like to call "mayhem magic."

After touring America, Robinson struck out for England, where he established himself as a popular Chinese conjurer with the public and the press. He had his detractors, those in the know who tried to expose the fact that he was not really Chinese, but an impostor. But one day he did them one better. He admitted publicly that the whole thing was a hoax.

Did the press and the public mind? Not at all. Robinson became more popular than ever. After all, he was the greatest magician in England. And magicians use the art of deception. So what was wrong with adding a little more deception to his act by altering his character and his background? So William Robinson carried on as Chung Ling Soo.

The highlight of Chung's performances was unquestionably the bullet-catching illusion. The effect is this: one or more bullets are fired at the magician and he catches them on a plate, he himself remaining unharmed. The illusion is dramatic, builds tension, and winds up with a sensational climax. All the ingredients of great theater.

Bullet catching is still being performed today, but rather infrequently — for good reason. It can be dangerous. There are several different methods of accomplishing the effect, and each one carries with it the risk of disaster.

Robinson would have the bullets marked for identification and checked by members of the audience before they were loaded into the guns. The bullets he caught on the plate were again checked and the markings were verified. Obviously, the bullets he caught would seem to have been the same ones that were fired from the guns.

If you think about it, you're bound to come to the conclusion that no bullets ever did come out of the barrels. And they didn't — usually. But on the fateful night that Chung Ling Soo was killed, one did.

At the inquest following the magician's death, the secret of his bullet-catching trick was revealed. His assistant, who happened to be his wife, had the bullets examined and marked while she was in the audience. While she mounted the stage she switched them for two other bullets with markings on them and handed them to the marksmen on stage. She then proceeded offstage. When she came back on later to hand the plate to Robinson, she slipped the original bullets to him under cover of the plate. When the muskets were fired he unobservedly dropped them on the plate — and the illusion was complete.

Which leaves the big question: why did the bullets in the guns *not* leave the barrels? The secret was in the guns themselves. Since they were muskets, gunpowder first had to be poured in from their muzzle ends. For the effect, a solid steel plug had been inserted in each gun to prevent the powder from reaching its final destination. Robinson also introduced other gimmickry into the muskets so they would produce an explosion and a flash of flame. But the bullets would never leave the barrels.

On that particular night, it was later found, a screw that held the steel plug in one of the gun barrels had worked loose, as a result of corrosion over a long period of time. A small amount of gunpowder had trickled down and was ignited when the trigger was pulled. The discharged bullet penetrated the magician's chest.

William Robinson, the great Chung Ling Soo, died for his art.

Ask anyone to name the greatest magician of all time, and chances are they will say "Houdini." After all, what other magic name has become immortal, and is even used in our everyday language to symbolize magic? On the other hand, ask that question of any magic historian and you'll get a different answer. For among magicians it is agreed that he was not the greatest all-round magician, but the greatest *escape artist*. In his less-sophisticated era Houdini's sensational escapes from bondage caught the public imagination more than did any of the great magical stage performers with their elaborate productions. To a good deal of the public Houdini was *really* a magician. His real secret of success was not just in the miracles he accomplished — it was in his ability to sell himself to the world. He was a master in garnering publicity.

Houdini was born Ehrich Weiss in Hungary, in 1874, the son of a struggling Budapest rabbi. As a baby he was brought to the United States, where his family settled in Appleton, Wisconsin. When he was fourteen years old the family moved to New York City, which eventually turned out to be very fortunate for young Ehrich. He got a job in a necktie factory to help support the family, but his mind was never far from magic. Out west he had learned some tricks from circus sideshow performers, and he continued to practise, becoming more proficient as time went on.

New York was the place for a budding magician to be at the turn of the century. He made contact with other practitioners of the art, discovered the magic shops, began to build a foundation for his future career. One day he discovered a book describing how to release oneself after being bound up by ropes. With some practice Ehrich mastered the method quite easily. Then he began to think ahead. Why not use an escape routine at the close of his magic act to make for a dramatic climax? He did it, and it worked. In his constant search for new effects he came upon an interesting combination escape trick. The magician would be placed inside a large sack, which would be tied up, then lifted into a trunk which would then be locked and tied up with ropes. A committee would come up onstage and inspect everything. The magician's assistant would then stand on the trunk, holding a large, curtained frame over her head, effectively blocking the audience's view of herself and the trunk.

Almost instantly the curtain would be dropped, revealing the magician himself on the trunk! The trunk would then be untied and unlocked, the sack with its human contents lifted out, untied — and there would be the assistant!

This truly astounding effect was later to be featured by Houdini under the title of Metamorphosis. And it is still being featured today by many performers.

Ehrich was also impressed by a book he had read by the great Robert-Houdin. So when he began to assemble a professional act and realized that he would have to adopt a stage name, he finally decided to borrow the name of the French master, adding an "i" to the end of it. With the addition of the "Harry," the immortal name was born — Harry Houdini.

He first worked with his brother, Theo, as a team. Their first escape trick had Theo fastened inside a crate, with Harry waving the magic wand while Theo escaped. After one performance when Theo couldn't get out, they reversed their roles and Harry became the escape artist. He never looked back after that.

When Harry was married, his new bride, Bess, became his stage partner, and together they worked the circus sideshows and tiny rundown theatres — wherever they could perform and eke out a living. Later he began the handcuff act that was to make him famous. There were many other magicians performing handcuff escape acts at the time, but Houdini was not content to be just another performer. He dreamed up something that had never been done before — the challenge escape. He challenged anyone, particularly the police, to bring their own handcuffs and fetter him.

Other performers tried to duplicate his feats, but couldn't. One by one they dropped out of competition. Houdini's challenges became more and more daring. He escaped from ropes, from chains, from handcuffs, from boxes, from trunks, from jail cells, and from combinations of all these confinements. His reputation began to spread.

In the year 1900 Houdini made the move that was to make him world famous. With Bess he sailed for England to perform in the land that was then the hub of the showbusiness world. Success followed success. Booking agents on the continent fought to engage him. He made a triumphant tour of Germany, where he became a sensation with his daring challenges and escapes.

In Russia he escaped from the infamous Siberian Transport Cell, an all-metal prison van used to move prisoners to exile. All this under the eyes of the secret police. He was the talk of Moscow.

Houdini had a sense of theater that was second to none. He was the first escape artist to realize that making it look easy was the wrong approach. He learned how to build up suspense on stage, to create the illusion that he was in grave personal danger. When you see this type of presentation on television today, remember that it was Houdini who established the trend almost a century ago.

When he was bound and manacled he actually could have freed himself in a few moments in many cases. Instead he would sweat and struggle for up to twenty minutes or more to release himself from the restraints. He would often be placed behind a curtain or in a cabinet. The audience would not see him struggling but would hear the sound of his efforts while the orchestra played some rousing music. He would then emerge, dripping with perspiration, triumphantly holding chains and handcuffs aloft, to thunderous applause. In fact, he often freed himself in a few minutes, sat behind the curtain rattling a few chains, then doused himself with some water, hidden away, to produce the "perspiration."

Things moved at a slower pace in those days. Today, an audience would not be likely to sit around waiting for the performer to reappear. He would probably emerge to find that the audience had disappeared. But in those simpler times they were content to enjoy the music and wait patiently for the miracle.

If that superb showman, Houdini were alive today, he would simply adapt to current standards. Knowing exactly what would attract the public, he took advantage of every situation, whether while performing on stage or while feuding with a rival performer in the newspapers.

As a youngster, he excelled in track and field and concentrated on building a powerful physique. He became an expert diver and swimmer, learning to swim underwater for long periods. He later went to work for a locksmith and became a master of the craft. This early training proved invaluable in later years when he was tossed off bridges into deep rivers while chained, locked, and jammed into sealed packing cases.

Houdini never left anything to chance. He was always fully prepared for any contingency. He had a handful of well-trained, reliable assistants who looked after every detail. To the public, Houdini was the miracle man that no locks could contain — but the miracles resulted from hard work, preparation, ingenuity and skill.

In 1910 he toured Australia and made headlines in still another medium. Airplane flight was then in its infancy. Only six years had passed since the Wright brothers had made their historic first flight. Houdini, the innovator and headline hunter, plunged into aviation. He learned to fly and had his own plane built. In Australia he flew it for the official measured mile, becoming the first man to success-fully fly on that continent.

Many people are not aware that Houdini also had a short career in the early movies. Predictably, he always played the daredevil hero who got out of tight situations and rescued the heroine in distress. He performed many of his famous escapes in these movies, and there were no camera tricks involved, as he insisted in doing the actual escapes as he performed them in real life. Many of these films are now in the hands of private collectors. Some have been shown at magic conventions I have attended — they are always a highlight of the program.

At the turn of the century spiritualism was at its peak, and after World War I the fake spirit mediums were out in full force, pretend-ing to receive messages from servicemen killed in the conflict. Houdini launched an all-out campaign against these charlatans. Some say he was bitterly opposed to these con-artists because, after the death of his mother, he had himself visited some of them, looking for solace. When, with his knowledge of conjuring, he saw through their deceptions, he was incensed and turned on them.

He exposed them by duplicating their effects and revealing their methods to the public. This opened up a whole new career to the great showman. Now he was receiving more publicity and reaping richer dividends than ever before.

But Houdini still had one unfulfilled ambition — to present a large-scale full-evening magic show. He finally produced this extravaganza and toured the continent, bringing the show to Montreal's Princess Theatre on October 18, 1926.

In his role as a spook-buster, he was usually called on for outside speaking engagements wherever he appeared. While in Montreal that October, he was invited to speak at McGill University one afternoon. The students jammed the hall to hear him lambaste the charlatans and reveal their methods.

In an earlier chapter I mentioned a telephone call I received when I participated in an open-line radio show in Montreal: the man at the other end of the line claimed he had been present at the events that led to Houdini's death. Well, when I eventually met with this gentleman, I received the entire story, authentic, and in detail.

The man's name was Sam Smiley, a well-known Montreal lawyer, still practising at the time we met. Smiley was one of the students in Houdini's audience that afternoon. He also had an affinity for drawing, and while the magician was speaking, Smiley sat there busily sketching the great man's profile. At the close of the lecture he approached Houdini, asking to have the drawing autographed. The magician declined, saying, "Come to my dressing room at the theater tomorrow morning.... . I'll autograph this if you'll make another sketch for me to keep."

So it was that Smiley found himself in Houdini's dressing room the next day, October 22nd, a witness to the events that would lead to tragedy. He had arrived with another student, his friend, Jack Price, and the magician welcomed them, then reclined on a couch while speaking to them and thumbing through his mail. He recounted some of his theatrical experiences while Smiley sat at the foot of the sofa sketching a portrait of Houdini.

Sketch by Sam Smiley of scene in Houdini's dressing room, Friday, October 22, 1926. Whitehead is at the left, Smiley at the right.

In Smiley's words, "At about 11 A.M. in walked this tall, sandy-haired man, about thirtyish. He was Gordon Whitehead, a McGill divinity student, returning a book Houdini had lent him. Whitehead was also an amateur boxer. After a few words he asked, 'Mr. Houdini, is it true you can take blows to the abdomen without discomfort, due to your superb condition?' Houdini, still looking through his mail, nodded absentmindedly. Without warning, Whitehead stood up and delivered several heavy blows to the magician's stomach area."

Smiley recalled, "Jack Price and I were shocked. He must have punched him three or four times. I remember Houdini gasping,

'That's enough, that's enough.' Jack Price asked Whitehead to leave, which he did." Houdini, a proud man, pretended to be unruffled and asked Smiley to continue drawing. The students finally left, saying goodbye to the magician, who seemed to be having no ill effects from his recent experience. This was not surprising to them, considering that here was a man who was renowned for his superb physique and his superhuman feats of skill and endurance.

After the punching episode Houdini began to develop acute pain but continued with his performances. He traveled to Detroit with his production, still suffering, but refusing to seek medical treatment. He finally collapsed backstage in a Detroit theater and was rushed to hospital. It was too late. Peritonitis had set in, and he could not be saved. He died on October 31, 1926, Hallowe'en — just nine days after the fateful blows were struck in Montreal.

The sudden demise of Harry Houdini was a major news story around the world. When Sam Smiley read the newspaper headlines of Houdini's death, he couldn't believe his eyes. "I couldn't sleep for weeks afterwards," he told me, "thinking about what had happened in that dressing room. I received a letter after Houdini's death, from his widow's lawyers in New York. They requested my affidavit as to the circumstances of his death. It had to do with double indemnity insurance. No criminal charges were laid."

Every Hallowee'en since Houdini's passing seances have been held to try to bring back the spirit of the magician. They have always failed. He has never been able to make his last great escape.

The Wonder Show of the Universe — anyone who was interested in attending magical theater in the 1920s or the 1930s was familiar with that production. It was the name of the fabulous magic extravaganza staged by Howard Thurston, America's greatest magician for almost three decades. Until his death in 1936 Thurston had only one rival in his field — Harry Blackstone. But Blackstone never really reached Thurston's level of prestige until the passing of that master magician.

Thurston, born in Columbus, Ohio, in 1869, studied for the ministry when he was a young man. Indeed, throughout his magic career he had all the manner and appearance of a man of the cloth rather than a showbusiness personality. Short of stature, with a dour visage and a serious bearing, you would never have taken him for a performing conjurer — until you saw him in action onstage.

Like many a magician, he was caught up in wonder at the art when he witnessed a performance by Herrmann the Great, one of the premier magicians of the turn of the century. From then on, the ministry was a thing of the past. Thurston set out on a career in magic.

He started out in a circus sideshow, where he was paid the grand sum of six dollars a week, and there began to learn his trade. Early in his career he developed an effect that was to become one of his finest — a simple and direct trick without any visible apparatus: the Rising Cards. He would hold a pack of playing cards in his left hand, motion above it with his right hand, and, one after another, several cards would rise out of the pack and float up to his hand.

The basic principle, which he invented, was to have an invisible thread stretched across the stage from one wing to another, with assistants controlling it. He initiated several refinements to make the trick easily workable and dependable. To the audience, the effect looked uncanny. This principle has since been adapted to accomplish many other stage effects.

Thurston used playing cards to produce another great effect. From the stage he would remove cards from a pack one by one, scaling each card into the audience. In the largest theaters he would be able to scale them with great accuracy to the farthest reaches of the balconies. This display of skill, although not actual conjuring, had an enormous effect on an audience. "Thurston cards" were kept for years by people who helped spread the word about the great magician.

Like Houdini and Chung Ling Soo, Thurston headed for England to make a name for himself, in 1900. He performed for royalty there and on the continent, then returned to America, continuing to develop and improve his presentation. Later he embarked on a world tour which included Australia and the Far East.

Howard Thurston's big break came when Harry Kellar, then America's leading wonder worker, decided to retire in 1908. Kellar introduced Thurston as his successor, and Howard took over

Kellar's elaborate production, a full-evening stage show. This was the beginning of the Wonder Show of the Universe, the show I witnessed more than fifty years ago in Montreal. Some of the effects have remained indelibly in my memory.

The curtain would open, revealing a giant-sized book at centerstage. Assistants would turn the huge pages, one at a time, each displaying the picture of a famous magician of the past. Then Thurston himself, in white tie and tails, would step out of the last page. One illusion followed another in rapid succession. Could anyone ever forget his Water Fountain? Thurston would move around the stage touching various articles with his wand. Wherever his wand landed, water would gush out in a fountain. He would touch an assistants fingertips, a foot, a head — from these, too, a fountain of water would spring out. He was also the first to perform the Vanishing Automobile. A small automobile would be wheeled onstage, filled with passengers. A puff of smoke, and the car and its occupants would disappear.

In my opinion, his greatest, most dramatic illusion was The Levitation of the Princess Karnac. I've seen dozens of versions of the floating lady since I witnessed Thurston's, but none has equaled his presentation in dramatic impact. He would place an exotically costumed female assistant under a spell, have her lifted onto a low platform, then cover her with a silk cloth. As the orchestra played appropriate music, the magician would gesture over the recumbent form, which would slowly rise. The platform would be removed, with the covered "princess" hovering a few feet above the stage. As Thurston gestured and intoned some words of command, the form would rise higher and float out over the orchestra pit. Then, as the music reached a crescendo, the magician, standing at the edge of the stage, would reach up and whip the the cloth away. The lady had vanished!

Many years later, on the Canadian Broadcasting Corporation's radio network program, "Morningside," I was doing a series on great magicians with actor-host Don Harron. We recreated that scene, complete with sound effects. That particular program received more enthusiastic approval than any other I had been on. For that I had to thank Don's acting abilities, and the genius of a super sound effects man.

I cannot recall if, in Thurston's version of this effect, the vanished lady reappeared in another location. This is the usual climax to this type of effect as you see it performed today. Which reminds me of a story that has been doing the magic rounds for a good number of years.

A magician was performing an effect in which his lady assistant was sealed in a cabinet with the usual fanfare, then, after the cabinet was reopened — zap — she was gone. A moment later she would reappear, running down the center aisle from the rear of the theater, shouting, "Here I am, here I am!"

Well, one day this miracle worker found himself performing in a town where he was staging his show in a theater that had another theater next door to it, the buildings being separated by a narrow alley. The neighboring theater housed a repertory company which, on that particular day, was presenting a dramatic play.

Now, during the magic show, after the young lady was locked into the cabinet, she was to make her usual secret escape through a trapdoor, run out the rear door backstage, dash down the alley, enter the theater, and run down the aisle, doing her vocal histrionics. On this particular day she zigged when she should have zagged. She mistakenly made a left turn instead of a right when she left the alley, entering the theater where the play was taking place instead of the one she had just left.

Just as the thespians on stage were enacting a dramatic death scene for a hushed audience, the magic gal came galloping down the aisle, yelling, "Here I am, here I am!" The result, of course, was chaos. Meanwhile, back at the other theater, the frantic magician almost had a nervous collapse after he discovered that his valued assistant had really disappeared.

Whether this story is true or not, I cannot guarantee. But it quite possibly is, because I have seen stranger things happen during magical performances, including some of my own — which I shall not recount.

In any case, it certainly was not during a Thurston show, because that master of the art was a perfectionist. Every facet of Thurston's performances was rehearsed and polished until it was faultless. And during every show his wife would sit out front making notes listing every detail that could be improved. For his dedication to the art and the many years he brought pleasure to the public, Howard Thurston will always hold a place as one of the greats of modern magic.

If you have ever seen magician David Copperfield on television, you have witnessed some pretty impressive illusions. From vanishing a jet aircraft to making the Statue of Liberty disappear, one would think he had established a magical record to shoot at.

Strangely enough, however, those feats were eclipsed more than four decades ago when a magician caused the Suez Canal to disappear, and magically changed the location of Alexandria Harbor — all without the benefit of television technology.

This conjuror was the famed Jasper Maskelyne of England, descendant of a long line of distinguished prestidigitators. His grandfather, John Nevil Maskelyne, was one of the pioneers who helped establish modern magic and who founded the London Magic Circle, still the elite of magical societies.

Jasper, the tenth generation of Maskelynes, was one of Britain's leading magicians when World War II broke out. His magical training and experience led him along a strange path in aiding the Allied war effort.

When he volunteered for service in the armed forces his age, thirty-eight, was a drawback. He had to pull a lot of strings to convince the authorities his magical skills could be put to practical use. He was not interested in merely entertaining the troops, as were most entertainment celebrities, but in serving directly in the army. A place was finally found for his talents in a Royal Engineers Camouflage unit. But he fought hard to have his own camouflage unit established, succeeded, and gathered a motley collection of experts who eventually created miracles never before seen on a stage or in a war. With these men under his command, Jasper Maskelyne came to be known as the War Magician.

The German armies under General Rommel were sweeping across Africa, had penetrated into Egypt, and were threatening Alexandria. The Allies were reeling — the situation was desperate. The British force at the port of Tobruk was all that prevented Rommel from reaching Alexandria when Maskelyne's unit got their first major assignment. They had to camouflage hundreds of tanks — a job that required ten thousand gallons of heat-resistant paint.

There was one problem: no paint was available. All they had to do was make it, out in the desert.

Resourcefulness, however, was Maskelyne's stock-in-trade. His crew finally created the paint — out of a base of camel droppings. He later admitted he couldn't have started lower than that.

But the magician's first really big challenge came when the top brass called him in and made a special request. It wasn't too complicated — just make Alexandria Harbor disappear.

The harbor was the supply lifeline for the British forces opposing Rommel. The German airforce was bombing it regularly, night after night. The situation was becoming critical. Something had to be done to camouflage the harbor, in some way.

Maskelyne saw that this concept was impossible. There was no way to camouflage an entire harbor, to make it disappear. But he immediately put his vast magical experience to work. There was another way — substitution — a basic principle of magical illusion. What he had done with human beings on stage he could do with an entire harbor.

In other words he would create a decoy by moving the entire harbor to another location. This seemingly harebrained scheme was finally accepted by the high command after persistent lobbying by the conjuror, and Maskelyne's magical crew got to work.

They found Maryut Bay, about a mile down the coast, where the contours of the coastline resemble the harbor's from the air. There they proceeded to establish an electrical network of wiring and lights paralleling that of the harbor at night. They built dummy ships and even set up explosives that would go off during a raid, starting fires that would attract more bombers. Alexandria Harbor, of course, would be blacked out every night, in the hope that the enemy bombers would be diverted by the lights of the substitute harbor.

That wasn't all. The Germans had been sending reconnaissance planes every morning to assess the previous night's damage. Maskelyne created heaps of rubble in the actual harbor area which would confirm that the Germans had been on target. He also persuaded the authorities to transfer most of Alexandria's anti-aircraft guns to the dummy harbor to strengthen the effect — a risky procedure, leaving the actual harbor almost defenceless if the ruse didn't work.

The entire operation was directed by Maskelyne each night from a master switching control board. It was his greatest magic feat to date. And it worked.

For eight nights the Germans plastered Maryut Bay and then finally ended their attacks. Alexandria Harbor was saved.

The British high command was impressed. Would the war magician attempt another bit of legerdemain? Simply make the Suez Canal disappear? "You see, Maskelyne, the canal is the most important link in our supply chain. The Jerries have to bomb and sink only one ship to block it. We'd like you to have a go at hiding the canal."

To Jasper Maskelyne, used to technical stage challenges, this was just another problem to be solved. It took a little time. He tried one magical idea after another with scale models. But he finally hit it — with optics.

How do magicians accomplish many of their feats? By creating a diversion with a flash of light and a puff of smoke. That's what did it, a flash of light — many flashes of light.

Maskelyne rounded up the limited number of searchlights around the canal and supervised the building of multiple reflectors around the searchlights — twenty-four fan-shaped reflectors welded to a steel ring around the lens. They sent twenty-four powerful beams nine miles into the sky.

After much experimenting, he mounted the reflectors on motors, which caused them to rotate at great speed. This created a fantastic, dazzling effect of whirling light that would virtually blind an approaching pilot. The whole system was put into service along the full length of the canal.

The Luftwaffe attempted to bomb the canal several times but couldn't get through the curtain of light. Jasper Maskelyne did it the magical way — with mirrors.

This principle was later used in Britain to protect likely targets from attack. It proved successful there, too.

Maskelyne's contributions to the Allied cause were numerous. He played a big part in the crucial battle of El Alamein when General Montgomery turned the tide in Africa — creating dummy tanks and guns — indeed, creating a fake diversionary army that completely deceived Rommel. Winston Churchill referred to this brilliant deception after the victory while speaking in the House of Commons.*

After the war Jasper Maskelyne found that stage magic was not in much demand in England. He and his family moved to Kenya in 1948, where he managed the Kenyan National Theatre.

The war magician died in Kenya in 1973.

The first time I saw The Great Blackstone and his Show of 1,001 Wonders was at the old His Majesty's Theatre in Montreal in the early 1950s. Unlike the time I had seen Thurston years earlier, I was now involved in magic myself and could observe another magician's performance with a more discerning eye.

Harry Blackstone made a great impression on me. When he walked out on stage you knew you were in the presence of a real magician — he just looked the part. Tall, erect, with his huge mane of white hair, and dressed in tails, he took immediate command of the stage. While the orchestra played, he removed his white gloves and tossed them in the air. They changed instantly into a live white dove that fluttered around. He then moved around the bare stage, gesturing with his arms. Wherever he motioned, a bouquet of flowers sprang up on the stage. In a few moments the stage took on the appearance of a huge garden, with a real fountain spouting water. From then on the magic continued for two solid hours until the audience was ready to believe almost anything.

Today, if you see the great magician's son, Harry Blackstone, Jr., performing in person or on television you will see some of the outstanding illusions that were featured by his father, and which he has adopted.

Two of his most famous illusions illustrated Blackstone's great showmanship. They did not require massive cabinets or hokey-looking apparatus. They were done with small, everyday artifacts, but had a powerful effect on the audience.

The Floating Light Bulb was one of these illusions. An assistant would bring a table lamp onstage. Blackstone would unscrew the light bulb. It would then light up in his hand, and he would release

---

*The entire story of Maskelyne's war effort is told in David Fisher's fascinating book, *The War Magician*, published by General Publishing.

it, causing it to float and move in the air under his direction, after passing a small hoop all around it. A very spooky effect.

His Dancing Handkerchief was similar, but even more puzzling and definitely more entertaining. Blackstone would leave the stage to join the audience and borrow a white handkerchief from one of the spectators. I can still remember his line at that point: "Thank you. It's just for showing, not for blowing." He would then take the hanky up to the stage, and tie a knot in one corner of it. Immediately the hanky seemed to take on life, squirming and wiggling in his hand. He would then release it, but it wouldn't fall to the floor. Instead it would remain floating and, as the orchestra began to play, it would dance all over the stage in time to the music. After a minute or so, Blackstone would grab the hanky and return it to its owner. A crowd pleaser if I ever saw one.

Blackstone's version of sawing a woman in two was superior to the usual effect as it was performed at the time. Most magicians would place the assistant in a box, then saw the box in half. Blackstone would have the hapless female lying on a platform in full view, and you could see the actual cutting take place.

She would be stretched out face down, and a motor with a huge circular saw attached could be seen suspended above her. He would slowly lower the assembly until the blade was touching her waist, flick a switch, and the motor would start up with a roar. The audience could then see the blade penetrating her body with a grinding noise. She would lift her head, let out a scream, and go limp. There were a lot of pale faces among the spectators. But the audience tension exploded into wild applause when Blackstone reversed the motor, raised the blade, and helped the revived young lady hop off the platform.

There is actually a certain amount of danger involved in this illusion if all the mechanical safety devices are not properly adjusted. A sick joke going around about this illusion is that it can be expensive for the magician if something goes wrong. He would have to book his assistant into two hotel rooms instead of one.

Harry Blackstone was born Henri Bouton in Chicago in 1885. He started out in vaudeville with his brother, Pete. Harry did the magic while Pete played the clown. Harry went on to develop a more comprehensive presentation with several assistants. Pete stayed with him as a stage assistant and general factotum backstage. The new stage name was supposed to have been taken from the famous Blackstone Hotel in Chicago, but Harry once told me, probably facetiously, that he borrowed it from the well-known American cigar.

In the 1920s he competed briefly with Houdini in the escape field, but didn't concentrate on that area for too long. He gradually developed his full-evening theater spectacular, The Show of 1,001 Wonders, which toured for years. After competing with Howard Thurston for several years, he took over as America's leading magical figure when Thurston died.

Blackstone's career stretched into the televison age. He made appearances on the Jackie Gleason comedy show and on many other programs, and continued to perform into his seventies. After he retired, he was honored at one of the giant magic conventions which I was fortunate enough to attend. He mounted the stage and performed a few of his peerless effects for about 1,500 magicians — probably his last public performance.

The Great Blackstone died in California in 1965 at the age of eighty.

Richard Cardini was the epitome of the "magician without apparatus." No other conjurer surpassed him when it came to the presentation of sleight-of-hand onstage. I emphasize "onstage," because there have been and still are some superb close-up manipulators in magic.

Cardini was born Richard Valentine Pitchford, in Wales in 1899. He served in the British Army in France during World War I, was wounded, and recuperated in hospital back in England. When he was in the trenches, young Pitchford had practised card manipulations whenever he had the opportunity. In hospital he asked for a pack of cards to pass the time and continued to develop his skills.

Back in civilian life he attempted to make a living as a conjurer in Wales, but without success. Moving to London, he obtained a position as a sales clerk at the magic counter of Gamage's department store. Still no work available as a performer. Working his way to Australia as a ship steward, he was finally able to get bookings in Sydney. His agent suggested adopting a good stage name. At that time names ending in "i" were popular with magicians — Houdini, for example. Pitchford's specialty was card manipulating, so why not Cardini? Thus was born an artist who originated a style of conjuring that was imitated by countless other magicians over the years — but never equalled.

Cardini worked hard to develop and hone an act that would eventually become world-famous. When he opened at the Palace on Broadway in 1927 the public got their first view of the finished product.

Cardini, impeccably attired in tails and wearing a silk hat, a cape, and white gloves, would walk onstage appearing slightly wobbly. He was playing the part of a British upper-class dandy out on the town, slightly tipsy and uncertain as to what was happening around him. As a fan of cards suddenly appeared in one of his gloved hands he would adjust his monocle with the other. Then more cards would appear as he tossed the first fan aside. He would gaze at them in bewilderment while they kept multiplying.

Suddenly he would see a billiard ball between the fingers of one hand. It would multiply until a number of them were displayed between the fingers of each hand. They would change color, then vanish. As Cardini was looking around to see where they had gone, a cigarette suddenly appeared between his fingers. He reached into the air, produced a lighted match and, with an unsteady hand, finally lighted the cigarette. He would then toss it to the floor, stomp on it, and another lighted cigarette would appear at his fingertips — and another, and another. He couldn't seem to put a stop to it. Finally, a lighted cigar appeared. A puff or two and he tossed it aside. As he walked offstage a huge meerschaum pipe appeared in his hand, which he puffed on after looking suitably astonished.

The entire act was performed in pantomime. The public never heard Cardini speak onstage. When I met Richard Cardini he had been retired for some time. He was a most gracious gentleman, and was always well-liked among magicians, who regarded him as a legend. He passed away in the 1970s.

Nate Leipzig was another sleight-of-hand expert who traveled around the world and played for royalty and heads of state. Born in Sweden, he was brought to the United States at an early age, and was raised in Detroit. He worked in the optical field, doing magic on the side, first as a hobby, then as a semi-profession.

From the beginning young Nate was interested mostly in sleight-of-hand with small objects such as thimbles and cards. When he eventually branched out into the professional field, he concentrated on performing at private engagements. His forte was close-up magic in the drawing room. His quiet yet engaging manner was a natural for this type of work, and his expert technique was impressive.

Although he did not think that his repertoire would be suitable for the vaudeville circuits, where the big money was to be made, on his first booking he was an instant success. You would not think that a magician doing card tricks and thimble manipulations could succeed on the stage of a large theater. But Nate Leipzig played the largest and most prestigious houses in the United States, Britain, Australia, and South Africa.

He used two techniques to accomplish this. First, he used the same style of presentation that he employed at private gatherings. He would have a committee from the audience come onstage and use them as a foil. They would actually represent the audience, but at the same time, even those in the balconies could get the drift of what was going on.

When he stood alone in front of the footlights to present his marvelous card and thimble manipulations, he made certain, in advance, that the lighting was excellent. His contracts always called for a powerful spotlight to be focused on his hands. Imagine a magician standing on a stage, manipulating tiny thimbles at his fingertips, and drawing applause from over a thousand people. Leipzig did it — for years.

And all this time he also kept to a busy schedule of private engagements, playing for the wealthy and the powerful, and for nobility. In 1907 he conjured for a private audience at Buckingham Palace: the king and queen of Denmark, the British king and queen, and the Prince of Wales. That performance brought him great fame: from then on he was showered with honors all over the world.

Nate Leipzig left us in 1939, but he also left a legacy of wonderful magical methods for other magicians to adopt. Many of his favorite and original tricks were published in Lewis Ganson's book, *Dai Vernon's Tribute to Nate Leipzig*.

Another of the great magicians of the past with whom I was privileged to talk and later to correspond was not known to the public as a magician at all. He was a world-renowned mind reader: Joseph Dunninger, master mentalist.

Born in lower Manhattan in 1892, Joe Dunninger was a contemporary and friend of Harry Houdini. At one time they were also competitors: Houdini and Dunninger both had popular full-evening magic shows. But Dunninger soon noticed that people were more impressed when he did a mental effect than when he pulled a rabbit out of a hat. So he gradually dispensed with the standard magic tricks and concentrated on mind reading.

In those days the usual mind-reading act consisted of a man-and-woman team, with the woman sitting blindfolded on the stage and her partner walking around the audience, picking up objects from them, then asking her to identify them. The trick was this: the man would identify each object using coded words. Dunninger, the individualist, would have none of that. He worked alone, using some proven effects and devising methods of his own. With showmanship and an ability to garner publicity second only to Houdini's, he began to build an awesome reputation as a man of supernatural abilities.

In the 1930s Joseph B. Rhine, the man who coined the term "extrasensory perception", was conducting his thought transmission experiments at Duke University. The press was giving the subject wide coverage and everybody was talking about ESP. The timing couldn't have been better for Joe Dunninger — and he didn't miss the opportunity.

He used the most ingenious methods to secretly obtain information. For example, when he was playing a theater in a particular city, he would obtain from the management copies of letters sent to the theater, requesting tickets. This gave him the names and addresses of many people watching his show, along with the seat number each person would occupy. Then he would arm himself with other little tidbits of information. He could discover anyone's car license number by having an assistant record it as the unsuspecting individual was parking his car and then follow him into the theater to see where he sat. Or he could identify the serial number of a ten-dollar bill that a spectator removed from his pocket — set up by the cashier who had handed the man his change when he purchased his ticket.

Dunninger had a vast array of mental effects that he could use to entertain an audience. But his greatest asset was his own personality. A successful mentalist has to have an excellent command of language. He has to radiate confidence and project a strong personality. Nobody, to this day, has ever topped Joe Dunninger in these characteristics.

Dunninger really hit his stride when he embarked on his broadcasting career in 1929. Radio was also just coming into its own, and Dunninger, as usual, was quick to take advantage of the new opportunity. He began a series of shows on WJZ in New York, but they didn't make much of an impression on the listening audience. He tried again in 1943, and this time he really connected. He began a regular Sunday-evening prime time show on the NBC network.

No mentalist had ever done this before. He became a sensation from coast to coast. He would read the minds of prominent personalities in distant cities, sometimes using methods that even other mentalists couldn't guess. Indeed, some of his methods, on air and in theaters, were so bold that other mentalists wouldn't have dared to attempt them. Who else would have the nerve to toss out an elastic-banded *gimmicked* deck of cards to an audience, asking the recipient to select a card and then toss the deck back? Dunninger did this and other such things with a degree of nerve and self-confidence that no other performer would approach.

With the arrival of television, Dunninger switched to that medium in 1948, with the usual success. At one time or another he had a series on each of the major U.S. networks, ABC, NBC, and CBS.

When I met Joe Dunninger in New York in the early 1970s he had retired because of illness. He used to drop in to Al Flosso's magic shop on 34th Street and spend an hour or two chatting about old times with Al and whoever else was around. It was there that we met and I absorbed some invaluable information from the old master.

I suppose there is a tendency by most adults, from middle age onward, to recall "the good old days." I, too, like to think back to the colorful and enchanting magical stage shows I witnessed and read about in earlier days. Perhaps they packed more impact because they didn't have to compete with the plethora of interests that occupy us now. Television, VCRs, computers, videos, movies we are in an age of information and entertainment glut.

But I do know this: today there are nowhere near the variety and quality of stage magicians that there were in the old days. This, of course, is because circumstances have combined to deny them the stages to perform on. And, let's face it, the professional magician is no longer as high on the entertainment totem pole as he was years ago. Times change, and so do public tastes.

7
Leading Magicians of the Present

I f you were to ask television viewers to name the leading magician in the world today, they would most likely say, "David Copperfield."

His annual magic specials are seen by millions. They are well planned, well choreographed, and well executed. He is young and attractive-looking and has an engaging personality. He is thoroughly dedicated to his art, and works hard at it.

David began conjuring at an early age: when he was twelve he was already getting paid for his efforts. Magic was his passion, but he was perceptive enough to develop other dimensions of his talents as well. Many magicians feel that it's enough to present tantalizing puzzles to their audiences. David realized that deception was only part of the presentation. To polish his act he studied theatre — acting, dancing, stagecraft.

As a youngster attending school in New Jersey, he would go into New York City after school almost daily. "I'd sneak into the Broadway stage shows every day," he once told me during a break between shows in Baton Rouge, Louisiana. "I'd wait for the intermission. I must have seen the second half of every show on Broadway. I would see them over and over again. I must have seen *Pippin* a hundred times." *Pippin* was the 1973 Broadway musical smash hit starring Ben Vereen, and it featured several magical effects. Since then David has become a close friend of Ben Vereen, who hosted Copperfield's China TV magic special.

David Copperfield onstage.

He directs all his shows himself — so he's much more than just a personality on camera or on stage. His magical vignettes — the charming little plays in which strange things happen according to a story line — are original Copperfield creations. They've become a trademark of all his shows, and provide a change of pace from the standard illusions.

The Copperfield illusion that probably caught the public imagination more than any other magical effect in years was his vanishing of the Statue of Liberty on television and in front of a live audience on Liberty Island. This feat not only raised the question "How was it done?" but also "How many magicians know how it was done?" Well, very few.

Says David, "Three hundred people were involved in creating and staging the illusion, but each was focused on only one small element. They never got the entire picture of the method. Fewer than five people really know the secret of this illusion." The feat was carried out like a secret military plan, where those involved are never aware of the entire operation.

The Statue of Liberty illusion cost over $500,000 to prepare — slightly more than it would cost to pull a rabbit from a hat. And it took months of cutting through red tape to finally get permission from the White House to pull it off. Perhaps they were concerned that David wouldn't bring the Lady back to Liberty Island.

As for the White House itself, David made several appearances in that hallowed hall for former president Ronald Reagan and his wife. His stage presentation has played the major show spots in North America, and he has won many awards as "Entertainer of the Year."

Among Copperfield's other television spectacles are effects like Walking through the Great Wall of China (performed as part of the China special) and the vanishing of a seven-ton jet aircraft which was sitting on the ground, surrounded by a ring of unbelieving spectators. He has also floated across the Grand Canyon, without benefit of visible support. All these on television, viewed by millions.

If I have one criticism of all Copperfield's presentations, it is that some of these feats are *too* miraculous. It is important, when presenting magic, to appear to be shattering the laws of nature. But the audience should be allowed a psychological *out*, some sort of possible explanation for the effect, even if it is incorrect. No rational person could believe that the Statue of Liberty actually did disappear — particularly when the feat is witnessed on television and even when the presenters say that no camera tricks are involved.

To some readers this criticism may appear to be professional nit-picking, but comments I have received from other viewers tend to bear out my opinion. However, this one drawback does not detract from the fact that David Copperfield is the leading magician of the day. Believe it or not, at the age of thirty-one, he has been seen by more people than any other magician in history.

At this writing, Canadian magician Doug Henning is no longer on the magical scene. He has given up his lucrative and popular conjuring presentations on stage and television and moved to India, where he has become involved in productions that put more emphasis on mystical things.

For several years it had been rumored that Doug had begun to believe that some magical effects on stage could be duplicated without using the usual mechanical devices — floating in air, for example. A discussion I had with him served to confirm that these rumors were based on fact. There was no doubt that he had developed a strong belief in the paranormal. The abandonment of his career and the adoption of his new vocation is further confirmation of his commitment to a new way of life.

Born in Winnipeg, Manitoba, in 1947, Henning was without a doubt the most commercially successful magician ever to come out of Canada. Because of television, he, like Copperfield, became a household name. He got his first big break in Toronto, after doing the usual circuit of kids' birthday parties and private entertainments. Along with another entrepeneur, he was able to raise several thousand dollars to mount a full-evening stage show which he presented at a Toronto theater. The successful production, called *Spellbound*, caught the attention of a couple of Broadway producers, who bought its rights, changed the name to *The Magic Show*, and took it to Broadway.

Doug Henning, along with the show, became an instant hit. *The Magic Show* ran from 1974 to 1977 — the first-ever magic production to establish such a record on Broadway — and it stimulated an interest in conjuring throughout North America. Henning himself established a new image for stage magicians. No more the white tie and tailcoat, the pointed beard and demonic look of the stereotyped conjurer. He dressed like a hippy and performed his tricks with a "gee whiz" type of childish enthusiasm. This fresh approach caught on with a new generation.

From the Broadway show Henning progressed to producing a full-evening theater presentation and an annual television special that put him in the front ranks of the profession. When I caught his live stage show in Toronto in September 1985, it had all the ingredients of a super production.

One of the ground rules for a good magic show is to start off with a bang. Henning did just that. From the opening number — in which Henning magically appeared through a sea of flames, produced his stage assistants from nowhere, and made a vicious-looking panther materialize — the show proceeded at a frantic pace from one illusion to the next. The audience was treated to every classic feat in the book — well, almost every one — in addition to several new ones which revealed the fresh concepts Henning and his staff had dreamed up. He also handled assistants from the audience faultlessly — finding some very attractive youngsters to enter into some magical byplay with him.

One of the most charming and magical moments came when Henning and his assistant-wife, Debby, sat together on a table with two handkerchiefs continually peregrinating between them, in and out of a huge glass bottle. This was a takeoff on Blackstone's classic Dancing Handkerchief, and a very entertaining one at that.

Henning's version of Sawing a Lady in Half was a real crowd pleaser. When he sawed two female assistants into sections and then "mistakenly" restored the bottom half of one to the top half of the other, it brought down the house.

Another good touch was Henning's use of TV camera projection. His close-up capers were shown on two giant screens. This allowed him to do some classy coin effects and other sleight-of-hand — and gave everyone in Toronto's huge O'Keefe Centre auditorium a clear view of the prestidigitation.

If there was one thing I would take issue with, it would be with his presentations of the classic levitation of a woman, and the floating silver sphere. Technically, they were well executed. But when Henning suddenly became the master magician, the man of mystery, he was out of character. The illusions somehow didn't ring true. Doug had established the character of the cheery guy-next-door who made strange things happen. He never could be a Blackstone or a Thurston.

All the same, Doug Henning displayed in his stage show an energy that was exhausting to observe. He was in every scene, disappearing from one place to appear in another throughout the performance.

Perhaps he will return to the world of conjuring one day. He is missed.

Does *The Magic Land of Allakazam* mean anything to you? If you watched television on Saturday mornings in the early 1960s it probably does. You could have been in Canada, the United States, Australia, New Zealand or Japan — you wouldn't have missed that show in any of these countries.

This fast-paced half-hour of magic was always performed in front of a studio audience packed with youngsters. And what was the magic word they would all shout out at the appropriate moment? All together now: "KELLOGG'S!" Fair enough, considering that the cereal manufacturer sponsored the program.

Mark Wilson, born in Indianapolis in 1929, was the star performer and the guiding genius behind the show. It had all the elements of good, clean television entertainment — just right for the younger set, and appealing to adults as well. The first weekly magic series to appear on network television, it ran for five years. For the first time in history, huge audiences were exposed to the great illusions of magic. This program really ushered in a new era in the art.

Even as a teenager Wilson had been interested in performing magic. But he was smarter than most. He didn't let the glamor of showbusiness blind him into relying on the profession for his bread and butter. He enrolled in university to study business administration and majored in advertising. It wasn't long before he used his newly acquired knowhow to advance his magic career.

After he landed the TV spot with *Allakazam*, he branched out in other directions while the show was still being aired. For the 1964 New York World's Fair, he created the Hall of Magic Pavilion and produced its shows for the General Cigar Company. This was only the beginning. He began to produce and direct exhibits for fairs in the United States and overseas for some of the largest corporations in the world — AT&T, 3M, General Motors, General Electric.

His company, Mark Wilson Productions, has also created live magic stage shows for amusement parks like Disneyland. He has trained magicians to appear in many of his productions — appearing personally only in major spots. Top television shows often use his services as a consultant. A plethora of illusions created by his technical staff jam his warehouse waiting to be leased to TV and film studios.

Mark Wilson has made his mark in magic and is probably the most commercially successful magician who ever lived.

You will recall my description, in an earlier chapter, of a magical effect I performed on a cruise ship, where I produced a number of light bulbs from my mouth. Well, that was only a minor variation on an effect originated by a magician who has lit up stages all over the world. Marvyn Roy, known as Mr. Electric in the trade, is one of magic's super specialists. A specialist is one who performs his entire act along one theme. With Marvyn the theme is light bulbs, which appear in and disappear from the most unlikely places.

Marvyn opens by producing, not cards or cigarettes, but small light bulbs from the air. They then light up in his hands. A large bulb held by a member of the audience lights up when the magician calls out a command. Then Marvyn holds a giant light bulb that suddenly lights up and just as suddenly goes out. He unscrews the socket end and pours an enormous quantity of milk out of the bulb. Another huge bulb is wheeled out on a stand and a lampshade is placed over it for a moment. The shade is removed, and there, curled up inside, is Carol, Marvyn's wife and assistant.

For his finale, Marvyn produces light bulbs from his mouth, as I did on the cruise ship. But his presentation is really sensational. Carol hands him a tumbler packed with small light bulbs. After he appears to swallow all the bulbs, he hands back the empty glass to Carol, then swallows a length of electrical wire for dessert. He then pulls one end of the wire from his mouth, and Carol grabs it and begins to back away. Out comes the wire, with the bulbs strung along it, all lighted. She keeps backing away, right across the stage, revealing *over thirty-five* bulbs! A sensational finish to a great act.

The genesis of this effect goes all the way back to Harry Houdini, who performed one like it in circus sideshows in his younger days. But Houdini "swallowed" sewing needles and thread instead of light bulbs, and he produced needles strung out on the thread. In later years some magicians accomplished the same effect with razor blades — I presented this one myself from time to time. But the use of light bulbs has certainly updated this presentation, and the Marvyn Roy version has never been matched.

Marvyn was born Marvin Levy in Los Angeles in 1925. Like many magicians he began performing at a very young age, and even then he seemed to believe in specializing. His first professional act, for which he was billed as Marvin the Silk Merchant, featured conjuring with colorful silk scarves. After service in World War II, he began to develop the light bulb act, and following the usual struggles to get bookings he finally hit it big: he was booked into the Palmer House's Empire Room in Chicago. He never looked back from there — working the best rooms in the largest hotels.

His performances on *The Ed Sullivan Show* brought him more recognition, and he travelled with Sullivan to perform in the Soviet Union. He also appeared in the London Palladium, at Radio City Music Hall, in Las Vegas — any place where they needed a class act. The fact that his act required no speaking made it easier for him to visit foreign countries, and he played many of them, from Turkey to Japan. Roy was always a favorite act of the late Liberace, and he often toured with him.

If anyone asked me to describe Marvyn Roy's magical performances in one word, I would have to say — electrifying!

He was known as The Man with the X-Ray Eyes. Khuda Bakhsh was born in a small village in Kashmir, high in the Himalayas. I knew him when we both lived in Montreal, but he never did reveal his true age to me. He left home as a teenager, travelling through Ceylon and Burma, developing the art of firewalking, which was very popular in those countries.

He later devised a way of doing the blindfold trick, which many magicians had been featuring — performing apparently impossible feats while blindfolded. Over the years many trick blindfolds have been designed, through which the magician could actually see. And many different methods have been invented to overcome the strictures imposed by scarves and eye coverings of various kinds. Khuda's early method, he told me, was a fairly simple one, but effective.

As a conjurer he worked on other forms of magical presentation, and in time he developed and mounted an illusion show which he eventually took to England. All this time he kept improving his blindfold effect, until it became his main feature and his trademark. He was now known as Kuda Bux, The Man with the X-Ray Eyes. The act became a headliner throughout Europe.

He would have members of the audience come forward to blindfold him. Under his direction they would place a large coin over each eyeball and tape them down. Then they would cover both eyesockets with a thick flour paste. The paste would in turn be held down by cotton wads that were also taped down. To top it off, gauze surgical bandage would be wound round and round his head many times, from the top down to his neck. No performer had ever before been subjected to such complete restriction. And remember, this was done by volunteers from the audience.

It seemed inconceivable that he could see through all these covers. Yet, once this was done, he would go into his act. A number of balloons would be strung up at one end of the stage. Kuda would be handed a rifle. He would point it at the balloons and fire again and again. Each balloon was demolished in turn. Someone would write something on a large blackboard set up on the stage. Kuda was handed the chalk, approached the board, and traced each figure that had been inscribed. He varied his stunts over the years, but always seemed to accomplish the impossible. Which is what a magician is supposed to do.

Is X-ray vision possible? I wonder what Kuda Bux would have done had he been confronted with the situation that tripped up a performer in New Orleans some years ago. This magician was in town for a theater engagement. He used the "blindfold drive," a stunt often employed to garner publicity before an engagement. The magician is blindfolded, sits down behind the wheel of a car, and drives through the busy downtown streets. The feat is well publicized in advance, of course.

This particular prestidigitator couldn't have been psychic, because he failed to take one thing into account. It was Mardi Gras season and the streets were crowded with people in a festive mood. Many were carrying huge clusters of balloons. Just as the blindfolded magician began to slip the car into gear with television cameras pointed at him, one reveller, in the spirit of good, clean fun, tied a cluster of large, opaque balloons to the hood of the car, effectively covering the windshield.

The drive ended before it began. It seemed that the superman's vision could penetrate the many layers of blindfold and the hood over his head — but balloons weren't his bag.

I am sure, however, that Kuda Bux, experienced showman that he was, would have found a way out of this dilemma. I like to think he would have grabbed his trusty rifle, stepped out of the car, and mowed down the balloons one by one.

Having known Kuda, I have often been asked by other magicians if I knew the method he used in his blindfold routine. I have had to say no. And I have never yet met or heard of any other magician who is in on the secret. I do know a few who claim to have an idea of how it might have been done, but they can't be certain.

Kuda Bux died in Hollywood, California, where he had retired, in 1981. As far as I know, he took his secret with him.

South America's gift to magicdom was Richiardi. Lithe, graceful, and handsome, the artistic Richiardi was another magician who made an impact on *The Ed Sullivan Show*, returning many times to that popular program.

His presentation of the Broomstick Illusion was a model of artistry, of how magic should be presented. Two assistants would come onstage, using the brooms to sweep the floor. The magician would take the brooms from them and then begin to suspend the young lady. It was apparent by his every studied movement onstage that Richiardi was a trained dancer.

His Vanishing Lady illusion was another classic effect that he revived from the last century and updated, to be shown on this century's state-of-the-art medium, television. This is the effect where a woman is seated on a chair, centerstage, and covered with a large sheet. You can see her outline under the sheet. The magician suddenly whips away the covering — and she's gone! With Richiardi's use of the proper music, and with his command of stage movement, the effect became a masterpiece.

I had a chance to see his nightclub act and meet him in Montreal some years ago. I never did see his theater stage show, but I have received many reports of this presentation, with particular references to his most sensational stunt, sawing a woman in half.

Like Harry Blackstone, he used a giant buzz-saw to do the dirty work. But Richiardi's presentation far exceeded Blackstone's in sensationalism, and, some say, in bad taste. First of all, when attendees approached the theater entrance they would see an ambulance parked at the curb. This immediately planted a sense of foreboding in some minds. During the sawing illusion that ambulance must surely have come to mind as the audience witnessed a horrifying spectacle.

The illusion was the closing one of the evening. It had to be. Anything else would have been anticlimactic after that. A large sheet of plastic was laid down, covering the stage floor. Richiardi would walk onstage, dressed in a white surgical gown, and approach the platform with the buzz-saw poised above it. Two assistants dressed as nurses brought a young lady forward. (Incidentally, she was Richiardi's daughter.) She was hypnotized in the usual manner and placed on the platform. The motor was started and the saw moved slowly, steadily, into the girl's body. Suddenly, what seemed to be blood spattered forth from the incision, all over the stage. The people in the front row of the audience could be seen to duck — half-expecting to be covered in gore. Richiardi stopped the saw, now blood-red, still imbedded in the girl's body. The audience sat dead silent, shocked.

The magician then stepped forward to the footlights, his gown now red-stained, and invited onstage any members of the audience who wanted to come up and inspect the situation. He was well aware of how people react at the scene of an accident. And sure enough, hundreds of people would line up in the aisles, mount the stage and walk in a slow procession past the inert form of the young lady on the platform — while the orchestra played slow, somber music. This unbelievable scene was like the viewing

97

of a corpse in a church funeral setting.

After the viewing, two assistants would lift up his daughter, support her still "unconscious" form under the armpits, with her feet dangling and her head hanging limp. Richiardi would step forward and inform the audience that it was "only a trick," and the curtain would come down. Definitely not your everyday, rousing closing of a conjuring performance.

Many magicians have criticized this presentation, but you can't argue with success. The Richiardi show played to packed houses all over the world.

Richiardi's untimely death at a comparatively young age came as sad news to magicians everywhere.

When I first saw Frank Garcia perform, it was on a theater stage in Montreal in the early 1950s. I can still see him pulling lighted cigarettes out of the air amid a thick haze of smoke. Since then our paths have crossed many times. And over the years I have learned a lot about magical presentation from him — from observation, from his advice, and from his writings.

In the trade Frank is known as The Man with the Million Dollar Hands. Knowing his sharp sense of humor, I have often kidded him about that tag line, but he usually tops me with a rejoinder of his own. Which illustrates one of his strongest points: the ability to entertain an audience not only with his skill but also with his wit and personality.

Born in New York City in 1927, of Spanish immigrants, his interest in magic began when he was about nine years old. He seemed to realize, even at that tender age, that practice and more practice was the key to success in conjuring. For the next few years he dedicated himself to developing his skills. Unable to afford costly apparatus, he invested his meager savings in one or two basic books on sleight-of-hand, and worked with playing cards and coins. The sacrifice and dedication of his early years eventually paid off.

Frank's father, a former merchant-seaman, had been pretty good at handling a deck of cards and playing poker. He taught his son some of the tricks of the trade at an early age, and Frank absorbed those lessons like a sponge. In later years he made a study of the many deceptions used by crooked gamblers. This eventually resulted in his bestselling book, *Marked Cards and Loaded Dice*, which has become one of the standard works exposing the methods of the gambling con-men.

In the meantime, Frank performed hundreds of shows, many times without pay, just to learn his trade. Eventually he developed his stage act and traveled wherever he could find bookings in the waning days of vaudeville. Then came the usual nightclub dates, working for, and learning to cope with, every type of audience.

Garcia always kept his contacts with other magicians. He loved the hobby part of the art, as well as the professional end of it. So whenever he could, he would spend time in the magic shops learning — trading ideas and quips with the other conjuring buffs. This eventually resulted in his being hired by Holden's, one of New York's leading magic houses at the time. At the age of twenty-one he became store manager. He finally gave up his business career to hit the road again and resume his performing career.

After some time in that uncertain branch of the profession, Frank made the decision that was to establish him as a leader in one specialty. He put together a gambling act, in which he would demonstrate all sorts of amazing things with cards and dice — then explain how they were accomplished. Instant success! He got more bookings than he could handle, and at high fees. He traveled all over the continent and appeared on most major television programs. Close-up conjuring, in the form of either card tricks or gambling demonstrations, is a natural on TV, with the camera zeroing right in on the performer's hands.

Now that his reputation as a gambling authority was well established, Garcia was in demand to give demonstrations to various law enforcement agencies. He worked with police departments in many cities, with the U.S. Federal Bureau of Investigation, with the Royal Canadian Mounted Police, and with the U.S. Defense Department.

Frank has never lost his interest in the art of close-up magic. In the trade, he is considered a leader in the field. Traveling constantly, he delivers lectures to magic groups — teaching and entertaining. He has written several books for magicians, each one concentrating on a specialty of the art, and has created several original and excellent magical effects that are now on the market. Frank Garcia has done more than his share in contributing to the knowledge and the pleasure of legerdemainiacs.

If you visited Las Vegas in the late 1980s, and took in the entertainment at some of the major hotels, you probably saw the sensational magic act of Siegfried and Roy. If not, there's a good chance you've seen them on television at one time or another. Considered by many to be the most successful magic act in history, that act is not soon forgotten once it's seen.

When the act was first presented in Las Vegas, it was held over for weeks, then months, then years. There's no doubt that, with all the headliners presented in that showbusiness mecca, Siegfried and Roy have established a record for longevity and sell-out performances. And no wonder. There has never been a magic show so spectacular — featuring illusions involving lions, tigers, elephants, and many other animals. Music, color, lasers, fog, fire, and female beauty are used to enhance every effect. Over one hundred entertainers are involved in the production.

The effects range from Siegfried performing solo magical effects to large-production illusions. The first sensational show-stopper begins when a huge African lion suddenly appears inside an apparently empty cage. It then disappears to suddenly be replaced by a leopard or a black panther. The cage is then covered, the cover instantly whipped aside, and there is Roy instead of the panther. While all this is going on, the beasts are roaring and swiping at Siegfried as he stands close to the cages — adding to the tension and excitement. There is never a dull moment in the whole show.

Siegfried Fischbacker was born in Germany in 1943. As a teenager he performed magic on German cruise ships for several years, under the stage name Delmar. On one cruise aboard the *Bremen*, in 1960, he met Roy Horn, also German, who was two years his junior. Roy was a ship's steward who had an affinity for animals and who happened to own a pet cheetah. But he could not take the animal on cruises because of ship regulations. On one trip he talked Siegfried into incorporating the cheetah into his act, which gave him the excuse he needed to bring the animal aboard. From these humble beginnings the Siegfried and Roy spectacular was born. Siegfried is still the magician; Roy is responsible for the handling and care of the animals.

Together they make a handsome and striking duo on stage. They travel the world between Las Vegas appearances, adding lustre to their ancient yet modern profession.

I first met Jay Marshall at the 1951 magic convention in New York City. I doubt that Jay has ever missed attending a major convention since that time — and I'm sure he's attended a lot of minor ones too. I know of no one so involved in the magic art as this professional performer, hobbyist, magic-book publisher and collector, and magic dealer. This variety of activity does not seem to have aged the man. Even in the late eighties, when Jay was approaching the age of seventy, he had the youthful appearance that only magicians can attain. After all, how *can* a person age when he keeps playing with toys?

Jay Marshall was another magician who appeared regularly on *The Ed Sullivan Show*, performing his faultless prestidigitation with the wry humor that only he could produce. He still maintains that tone today.

Walking out on stage he introduces himself as "one of the better cheaper acts," then proceeds to amaze his audience with some deft conjuring, always was accompanied by a few casual, humorous, self-deprecating remarks. The highlight of his act always was and still is Lefty — a white glove that the accomplished ventriloquist wears on his left hand. With a couple of black buttons for eyes and two extensions for ears, the glove looks like that old magician's companion, a rabbit. When Jay works his left thumb up and down, the mouth seems to be moving, and when he begins his ventriloquial conversation with the glove, you would swear that Lefty has come to life. It is masterful entertainment, particularly when Lefty breaks into song with his hilarious rendition of "If I Had My Way." I can still see Jay Marshall standing alone in the spotlight on the gigantic stage of New York's Radio City Music Hall, holding an audience of thousands in the palm of his hand as he carries on a conversation with his other hand. *That* is showmanship!

Lefty was born during World War II. When Jay was serving in the army, he was pressed into entertaining the troops, but found it impractical to be packing and transporting his wooden dummies from place to place. So he devised the glove puppet as a partner.

What could be more portable? Lefty stuck with him when he resumed his professional career after the war.

Marshall played all the leading nightclubs and theaters in America and Europe and acted in a Broadway play, *Love Life*, for good measure. He was a television pioneer, first appearing on that medium in 1940. Since then, of course, he has had a long career on hundreds of TV shows.

With his wife, Frances (who has been a well-known writer and performer in the magic field for years), Jay operates the Chicago-based magic company, Magic, Incorporated. They publish magic books, operate a retail shop, build equipment, and do a roaring mail-order business. Their building also includes their home — and the living quarters are hard to distinguish from the business section. Books are stacked almost to the ceilings wherever you turn.

Jay Marshall is the magic buff *par excellence*. You'll never see him happier and more enthusiastic than when he is at a magic convention mixing with other magicians. Which probably explains why he is held in such affection by his peers.

Carl Ballantine, billed as "The Great Ballantine," was in a class by himself — once seen, never forgotten. He performed magical effects that didn't work. Need I say more? If you ever caught his act on television, you know exactly who I mean, even if you didn't remember his name. I have seen his act many, many times, on stage and on television. I can recite his every line, recall his every movement. And yet I have never failed to be entertained, even when I knew what was coming next. There was magic to his magic.

Carl didn't walk on stage — he strode out. Tall, supremely confident, dressed in tails, he approached his prop table at centerstage with long, purposeful strides. He beamed at the audience with an expression that said, "Relax folks, the master magician is here — I'll take charge now."

He would pick up a piece of rope and a pair of scissors, cut the rope in two with a flourish, wave over the two pieces with an even greater flourish, and command them to be restored into one length again. Nothing happened. Carl would scowl, toss the ropes aside, peer backstage, and yell, "All right, who's been fooling around with my rope?" This set the stage for the rest of the act. As everything went wrong, the magician would sometimes get frustrated and sometimes toss off a side remark to cover his chagrin — but he would never, never lose his confidence.

He always had a tophat sitting open-end up, on his prop table. "Now," he would proclaim to the audience, rubbing his hands together, "get ready for the magic rabbit." Then he would address the still unseen rabbit, while looking down into the hat, "All right, here I come." He would reach into the hat and grope around, a surprised look suddenly appearing on his face. Then he would reach down further, and further, until his arm disappeared from sight, right up to the armpit. The audience would dissolve into laughter at this point, as it was obvious that the tophat had no top, and he was reaching down inside a gimmicked table. Finally he would withdraw his arm with a look of triumph on his face — clutching a limp-looking rubber chicken, which he tossed disdainfully over his shoulder before going on to the next non-magical effect.

The act was always a hit on television, but Ballantine's live stage performances packed an even greater wallop. When I saw him at the famous Palace Theater on Broadway he brought a jaded New York audience to life. His act demonstrated perfectly that "it's not what you do, it's the way you do it." In lesser hands, the thing would have bombed. But Carl created an onstage character which, combined with his natural personality, came up a winner.

In earlier days he had a standard magic act that didn't get too much notice. Then one day he came up with the idea for this new character, and hit the jackpot.

To do his type of act, Ballantine has to be an accomplished actor. And he has proven that many times over. If you have ever seen that excellent series, "McHale's Navy," which ran on television for years, you will remember Carl as the lively character who was always scrounging up things for his buddies. He has also appeared in other vehicles, both comedic and dramatic.

But it is as The Great Ballantine that Carl has made his mark in magicdom.

One of the greatest of living magicians is a man barely known to the public. Dai Vernon, known as "The Professor" to more than one generation of magicians, began his professional career as a

103

stage performer, but then gave that up to concentrate on his real interest, close-up conjuring.

Since there was not a great demand for this form of presentation in the entertainment market, Vernon nearly dropped out of sight as a theatrical presence. Using his immense skills, he did entertain at the tables in some of America's leading nightclubs and at prestigious private gatherings, but for most of his professional career, he concentrated on teaching the art of conjuring to other magicians. He taught private lessons, lectured to magic clubs and at conventions, wrote books and made videos on the subject, imparting the methods of what is known as "the Vernon touch."

David Verner was born in Ottawa, Canada's capital, in 1894. As an amateur magician while still in high school, he took the name of Dai Vernon, which sounded more "showbizzy" to a young magician. He actually began doing card tricks when he was much younger, and was always more interested in sleight-of-hand than in using tricky apparatus. He realized at an early age that the real secret of digital deception was to make every move seem natural, not to arouse suspicion. That eventually became the basis of his teaching methods.

In his twenties, Vernon began to explore the New York market, making contact with the big city magicians and learning from them, just as I did many years later. But with Vernon there was another side to the coin. The New York magicians also learned a lot from *him*. He had already developed original methods with cards and coins and other small objects that amazed some of the American experts.

Strangely enough, Vernon had to turn to another of his skills to earn a living at that time. He had become proficient at silhouette cutting — cutting out people's profiles on black paper. He plied his trade at Coney Island and other places where the public gathered.

Later, he developed a polished stage act which he performed at places like the Rainbow Room at New York's Rockefeller Center and at Radio City Music Hall. These performances won critical, but not public, acclaim. So Vernon reverted to his presentation of intimate magical entertainment and stayed with it for the balance of his career.

Dai Vernon is at his best, and is happiest, when teaching other magicians. Many years ago I was instrumental in bringing him to Montreal to lecture for a gathering of magicians from Montreal and Ottawa. I still have the movies I filmed of The Professor performing his own inimitable version of the Cups and Balls. He has since published the method and the technique he used in that classic trick, but to see the master in action was a treat not soon forgotten.

In the later years of his active career, he was in constant demand to lecture at the big magic conventions. Most often he would be scheduled to deliver special midnight lectures. Speaking to standing-room-only audiences, he would go on for hours, teaching the psychology of presentation, showing sophisticated sleight-of-hand moves, and answering questions on all phases of the art.

The Professor has spent the last few years of his retirement practically living at the Magic Castle in Hollywood. There he is the sage in residence, always willing to talk over old times and dispense magical advice.

Dai Vernon has made an enormous contribution to the advancement of the art of conjuring. He is a living legend.

Some Canadian magicians, like Doug Henning and Dai Vernon, have made big names for themselves after moving to the United States. But some topnotch, internationally recognized Canadian conjurers have chosen to remain in the land of the maple leaf while practising their prestidigitation.

Sid Lorraine is one such magician. Born Sidney Richard Johnson in England in 1905, he was raised in Canada, and has been a Toronto resident most of his life. He adopted his stage name while he was still a youngster beginning to dabble in magic.

Sid is a man of many parts — a commercial artist, a magic magazine columnist for many years, a creator of magical effects with many tricks on the market, an author of several books on magic, and a performer who has always been a favorite at the big national, American magic conventions. His forte has always been novelty and humor — whether in writing or in performing. His books always stress the patter, or verbal communication, that must be integrated into the presentation of a trick. And his personal presentations are living proof of his philosophy. They are packed with novelties of his own creation and a witty humor that has endeared him to generations of magicians.

To Lorraine, magic has always been a hobby, and his efforts have always been directed to the advancement of the art. Sid Lorraine is a Canadian magical national treasure.

Another Canadian magician, who sadly is no longer with us, was John Giordmaine. Born in Malta, John also spent most of his life in Toronto. His specialty was entertaining children, and no performer I have seen has even come close to matching his competence in this field.

Short of stature, with a round, jolly face, he was the prototype of a kids' magician. Which is not to say that he couldn't handle an adult audience too. He was adept at any type of presentation.

Giordmaine left you breathless. Where other magicians would do three tricks in fifteen minutes, John would do fifteen tricks in three minutes. His patter proceeded at the same rate; there was never a dull spot in a Giordmaine act. I can still recall seeing him captivating an audience of 1,200 magicians at a magic convention. He would stagger out on stage, carrying a huge garbage can almost as big as himself, clump it down at centerstage — then go on to perform trick after trick at a dizzying pace, tossing each article into the can when the trick was concluded. At the finish he would drag the can offstage while the audience erupted into applause.

For many years John ran the magic counter at the huge Eaton's department store in downtown Toronto. It was there that he made contact with the young budding magicians of that metropolis and got many of them started. Indeed, he was an inspiration to me when I saw him perform at a Christmas show at the Eaton's store in Montreal, when I was still a neophyte in the art. I didn't dream then that we would later become friends.

John Giordmaine will be remembered not only as a fine magician, but, by those who knew him, as a most likable human being.

Ross Bertram is definitely not a household name, and few members of the public would ever associate him with the magic profession. But among magicians around the world, Ross Bertram is recognized as one of the profession's leading sleight-of-hand experts — particularly with coins.

I first saw him work at (you guessed it) the 1951 New York magic convention. His coin conjuring simply blew my mind. The man performed miracles. Coins would vanish, change places, appear from nowhere, and change from silver to copper to gold. And here I was sitting across a table from him, only three feet away. When it came to close-up magic he was the talk of the convention.

It wasn't until years later, when I read his writings on magic, that I learned how he accomplished some of his amazing effects. He was able to deceive even knowledgeable magicians because so many of his sleight-of-hand tricks were original. With such skill and originality, the onlooker didn't have a chance to spot his unique methods.

I should point out that reading about the methods used by an expert like Bertram doesn't immediately make the reader a master of the author's effects. This would require long hours of practice and dedication. Or, as Jay Marshall would say, "years of dedication and self-denial." To read the revelations of a skilled sleight-of-hand expert is merely to satisfy one's curiosity. To go further you simply must work at it.

Ross, another Torontonian, was born in Canada in 1912. He performed for the public for a number of years, working close-up at Toronto's Royal York Hotel from 1934 to 1953. He also worked the trade shows and performed on many TV programs. An expert with cards, he is equally adept with dice and other articles associated with gambling. At one time he appeared on a number of television shows demonstrating deceptive gambling techniques.

Many years ago, however, he decided to give up all public performing and concentrated, as did Dai Vernon, on doing magic for magicians. But Ross has always been a relatively private person, so he never did go on the lecture circuit. This tendency to privacy has kept Ross Bertram out of the public eye for years. But his writings remain — a rich legacy to be passed on to future generations of conjurers.

It occurs to me, as I wind up this part of the book, that I might be accused of male chauvinism. I have described female assistants to famous magicians, but not once have I referred to an actual female magician. They do exist — although the field has so far been dominated by men — and some of them have made a mark as professional conjurers, past and present.

Adelaide Herrmann was without a doubt the most famous

professional woman magician who ever lived. Her career spanned almost fifty years, at the turn of the century. She first appeared, doing her own act, in the stage production of her husband, The Great Herrmann. They toured the world — one of the great magic shows of their time. When her husband died, Adelaide continued on her own as a vaudeville headliner for at least thirty years.

Another famous female magician from the past was an English lady named Mary Ford, known professionally as Talma. She was a rarity — a female magician who specialized in sleight-of-hand with coins. Indeed, she was known as the "Queen of Coins." She had another claim to fame as the first person to be levitated in the air and then vanish. This effort was known as the *Asrah* levitation; it was used later, as I have described, by Howard Thurston. Talma was married to another renowned conjurer, Servais Le Roy, who was the inventor of Asrah, and they too toured the world with their marvelous production.

Jane Thurston was another magic lady who made a name for herself on stage. Magic was in her background — she was the stepdaughter of the great Howard Thurston. After she was trained in the art, her own act, which included song and dance, became a feature of the Thurston productions. When Thurston died in 1936 Jane retired from the stage. She did not perform again until many years later when a magic convention in Boston staged a Tribute to Thurston, in which many of his old illusions were revived. I was in that audience when Jane Thurston received a standing ovation for her brief return to the stage.

The first female magician I ever met, and saw perform, was Celeste Evans, an attractive young woman who came from a small town in British Columbia. That was at the time I was involved with Ring 62 of the International Brotherhood of Magicians in Montreal. Celeste had already developed a professional act and was touring Canada, playing the small clubs. She contacted me when she arrived in Montreal, and I invited her to one of our club meetings.

At the time, this was quite a novelty for us all-male magicians — a female conjurer! She volunteered to magish for us, and we all indulgently yielded, then sat back with a critical eye. As I recall, her performance didn't make too much of an impression. It did not yet have the polish of a really professional presentation.

It wasn't until a few years later that I received any news of

Celeste Evans's career. She must have done something right, because she was now being booked by a New York agent, and eventually toured the world with her act. As a matter of fact, she reached the point where she was considered to be the leading female magician of her day.

There are other woman conjurers on the scene today, but relatively few, as compared to men. In a field always dominated by men, the ladies do not seem to be interested in mounting a challenge for prominence. When you consider that they have succeeded in establishing themselves in just about every other branch of showbusiness, the question arises, why not magic?

I have consulted my crystal ball, but the answer has not revealed itself. I do know that magic conventions attract as many females as they do males, so certainly the interest is there. My own magic classes, too, have always included a few women — and often they were the brightest of the students. But, as active performers, amateur or professional, their numbers are thin.

III
Magic for Everyone

Introduction

The magical effects in this part of the book are designed for the beginner. At the same time they are quite effective. If you would like to call yourself a magician you should really learn to perform some of the tricks in this section. But remember, this will just get you started. I have chosen these particular effects for a specific reason. They are all easy to do, and do not require expensive apparatus.

Why easy to do? Because nothing is more discouraging for a neophyte than to plow through a magic book containing muddy directions for difficult sleight-of-hand moves that would require the skills of an expert — or as many fingers on each hand as an octopus has tentacles. I speak from experience.

For those of you who are encouraged to go further in magishing, there are countless excellent magic books on the market. There are books on specialty magic: coins, cards, sponge balls, cups and balls, mentalism, newspapers, ropes, and so on. There are books on magic tricks in general, some more advanced than others. And there are books describing how large stage illusions are made up. These last will appeal mostly to the curious.

Some magic books can be found in libraries, others are available only in bookshops. The greatest variety, of course, will be found in the magic shops in your area. And the magic shop manager will be able to give you the best advice on which book to purchase.

You will notice that some of the tricks in the following chapters include quotations for magicians to use when presenting the effects. These remarks are included only as a guide. Please do not use them verbatim. The first rule of presentation is to be yourself, so use your own form of expression.

Most amateur magicians are interested in using effects with playing cards and with money, because you can find a deck of cards, a few coins, or some paper currency almost anywhere. There is nothing odd about these items — people see them every day — so when you make them do strange things, it does look magical. I have, of course, covered magic with cards and money, but if you want to progress in these specialties I would strongly recommend purchasing a basic book on card or coin manipulation. Again, visit your local friendly magic shop.

In order to present the following magical effects with the most impact, I would suggest that you read the last chapter before you even look at the tricks. Then read the tricks, then read that chapter again. That's where you will find the real secrets of the art of conjuring, advice too often ignored by the average amateur.

Magicians have always had a way of estimating the worth of a book on magic tricks: if it contains three or four tricks that are practical and useful, they are worth the price of the book.

I hope you can find three or four tricks in *this* book that are useful to you. Happy magishing!

8
Card Tricks

Presto-Reverso

What the audience sees: Have someone select any card from a deck. Say it's the ace of hearts. Hold the deck face down in your left hand and have them place the ace face up on top of the deck.

Say, "I will now place this card face up in the middle of this deck and it will disappear."

Place the ace in the middle of the deck. Wave your right hand over it. Spread the cards again: There will be a card face up, but it won't be the ace of hearts — it will be the 5 of clubs!

Next, place the 5 card face up on a table and hand the deck to someone, saying: "Would you look for the ace of hearts?" They will be surprised to find that the card has vanished!

Next, take back the cards, hold the deck face up and place the 5 card back into the middle of the deck, also face up. Turn the deck over and wave your, hand over it again. Spread the cards. Presto! There is the ace of hearts again, face up in the middle of the face-down deck. Magic.

Preparation: Reverse two cards and place them face up at the bottom of a face-down deck. Take a tiny bit of beeswax, or any other sticky material, and place it at the center of the back of the bottom card.

How the trick is presented: After the ace of hearts is selected, lower your left hand to your side and reverse the deck. The sticky card (the 5 of clubs) is now on top.

When the ace of hearts is placed on it, press it down so that they stick together. You will remove the two cards as one and place them into the deck.

As you are telling the audience that the card will disappear, lower your deck to your side again and turn it over.

As you bring the cards up, pull out the bottom card with a swinging movement (so nobody will notice it was reversed) and say, "This isn't your card, is it?" Then place it back face down.

When you place the 5 card on the table, the ace will be stuck to it, face down. It will look like one card and be replaced that way. When you show them that the ace is back in the deck, simply pull it away from the sticky 5 card.

Practise all this. It will become clear.

Black Magic

What the audience sees: Have someone shuffle a deck of cards, then tell him, "When I turn my back, please remove an even number of black cards from the deck, any number you wish, and place them in your left jacket pocket.

"Now, deal the remainder of the deck into two equal piles, face down."

When this is done, ask your assistant to shuffle each pile of cards separately, then replace them on the table.

Then say, "Please choose either one of those packs and remove all the black cards from it. Place them into your right jacket pocket. Hold onto the red cards for now.

"I will now perform my little miracle."

Turn around, pick up and look through the remaining cards on the table, put your hand to your forehead and say, "Let me think. I would say you have 12 black cards in your left pocket and 7 black cards in your right pocket. Please check."

To everyone's astonishment, you will be absolutely correct.

"It's easy," you explain. "Black magic."

How the trick is presented: In this case, let us suppose there are

12 cards placed in the left pocket and 7 in the right pocket.

All that you have to do when you pick up the remaining pile are a few simple mental calculations. Look through the cards and see how many red cards you have and how many black cards.

Suppose that you have 13 reds and 7 blacks. To the number of black cards (7), mentally add twice the number of red cards (26), giving you a total of 33.

From 33, subtract the number 26. This gives you 7.

This reveals the number of black cards in your assistant's right pocket.

Now, if you mentally add this 7 to the 7 black cards you are holding, you get 14. Since you know that a deck of cards contains 26 black cards, subtract the 14 from 26 and you know there will be 12 black cards in the left pocket!

This formula works with any numbers.

Be sure that you are very clear when you instruct your assistant in what to do because, with your back turned, you cannot check his actions.

This is one trick you can repeat if your audience insists.

Jumping Card

What the audience sees: Have someone select a card from a deck. Then say, "Please show your card to everyone and remember it. Now, please hand it back to me face down so I can't see it."

Take the card and insert it in the middle of the deck. Hold the deck in your left hand, vertically, so that the faces of the cards are towards the audience.

Say, "You, know, it's strange, but you have selected the only card in the deck that practises gymnastics. This card can actually jump in the air.

"Would you like to see it happen? All right, call out the name of the card and watch."

When this is done, nothing happens. Say, "Oh, I'm sorry. You must name the card and then call 'JUMP'." Still nothing happens. Then you say, "It's really my fault. I forgot to tell you. You must say *please* jump." When the spectator calls out these instructions, presto, the chosen card jumps right out of the deck.

Preparation: If you don't wish to damage a couple of cards from a good deck, take two cards from an old deck with the matching backs. Take a small rubber band and cut it. Staple one end to the center of each of the two extra cards. The total length of the rubber band should be about five centimeters (two inches) after it is stapled to the cards. Place these cards in the middle of the deck.

How the trick is presented: When you hold out the deck for a card to be chosen, just spread out a few cards in the top half, so that no one will pull out one of the two gimmicky cards. When everyone is looking at the chosen card, spread the middle of the deck very slightly so that you can see where the two secret cards are. Then, when you take back the selected card, just slide it between the two cards joined by the rubber band and push down on the rubber band. Then hold the deck tightly in your left hand. Whenever you wish it to fly out, just release your grip slightly — and away it goes.

Quite a surprise. But don't forget to concentrate on the showmanship.

Spell-a-Card

What the audience sees: Have someone select a card from a deck, remember it, put it back in the deck and then shuffle the cards. Take the cards from her and say, "I'm going to attempt an impossible feat. What was the card you chose?"

When she calls out the card, say, "I'm going to remove one card at a time and spell out your card with each one I remove." (By "spelling out," you mean that each card removed represents a letter of the chosen card — e.g., A-C-E-O-F-C-L-U-B-S.)

"The last card will be the one you chose. But to make it more difficult, I'll place the deck in my pocket first and do it blindly.

You then proceed to do as you said — and the last card will prove to be the chosen one!

Preparation: Take a second deck which has the same backs as the original and divide it into four packets, one for hearts, one for hearts, one for diamonds, one for clubs, etc. Arrange each suit in order (Ace, 2, 3, etc.) Place each packet into a separate pocket.

How the trick is presented: After the card is named, you will know the suit. Place the deck into the pocket that already contains the packet of that suit. Now, begin removing one card at a time from the packet, spelling out the chosen card. The cards in the packet are in order, which makes it easy to find the selected card, which will be the last one you remove.

Two important things to remember: When you place the packets in your pockets before you begin the performance, be sure to lie them down on their side edges. Then, when you place the full deck in your pocket, have it standing up on end. That way, you can feel the packet separated from the full deck when you are pulling out the individual cards from the packet.

Or if you wish, you can place a small, cardboard divider in each pocket beforehand, to keep the two card sets separate.

Secondly, when you remove the cards for the spelling effect, it's important to lay them on a table face down, so that your audience doesn't spot that they are all from the same suit.

Timely

What the audience sees: Look at your watch and ask everyone else to check theirs. Then announce the time.

Let's say it is 4:25. Ask someone to write it down. Then hand a deck of cards to a spectator and say, "Please shuffle the cards and remove any six of them."

After this is done, say, "Now please deal out the rest of the deck into two face-down piles, alternating from one pile to the other as you deal.

"All done? Will you now select any card you wish from the six cards you put aside, remember it, and then put it on top of these two piles... then place the remaining five cards on top of either pile.

"Now place the pile which does not contain your chosen card on top of the pile that does. Thank you."

Look at your watch and say, "That didn't take too long. By the way, what time was it when we began this little miracle?" Someone will check the note written earlier and call out, "It was 4:25." "4:25?" your repeat. "All right, what happens when you add 4 to 25? You get 29, right? Would you please count down 29 cards from the top of the deck?"

When this is done, the 29th will be the chosen card. A timely effect.

How the trick is presented: There is one thing to remember about this trick. It can only be done at certain times of the day. Jot down these times and keep the note handy: 1:28, 2:27, 3:26, 4:25, 5:24, 6:23, 7:22, 8:21, 9:20, 10:19, 11:18, 12:17.

You'll notice that if you add the hour to the minutes, you will always get a total of 29. And the arrangement of the cards will always place the chosen card 29th from the top. Like many tricks, this one is so simple and yet so puzzling. Just make sure you check your watch and get ready to begin at just the right time.

Ring-a-Card

What the audience sees: Shuffle a deck of cards, remove the four Queens, and place them face down in a row on a table top. Then ask someone to cut the deck in half. Place the bottom half crosswise over the top half.

At about this time, the telephone begins to ring. For each ring, point to one of the Queens in turn, until the phone stops ringing.

Suppose that when it stops ringing, your finger is on the Queen of Spades. You say, "Please remember the suit — spades."

The telephone will now ring again. Suppose it stops after 6 rings. You then say, "Six rings?" That must be the 6 of spades. Please check the bottom card of the top pile.

It will be the 6 of spades!

Preparation: Arrange for a friend to call you at a certain time. Decide on the number of rings and the order of the Queens on the table. After she has rung the number of rings for you to choose the Queen you want, she will hang up and dial again. The number of rings this time will correspond to a certain card that you have decided beforehand and placed carefully in the deck.

How the trick is presented: About a minute before the arranged time for the phone call, begin spreading out the Queens and have the deck cut. When you are looking through the cards to find the Queens, look for the card you have decided will be the chosen card and casually place it at the bottom of the deck.

Now, when the deck is cut, that card will automatically be at the bottom of the top pile, placed crosswise over the bottom pile. It really doesn't matter where the deck is cut, as you can see.

Coded Cards

What the audience sees: Ask a spectator to shuffle a deck of cards. Take the deck and place it on a table. Write something on a slip of paper, fold it, and give it to someone to hold. Let's call him Joey.

Write something on another slip of paper, fold it, and hand it to a second person. Let's call her Laura.

Give the cards to Laura and ask her to deal any number of cards on the table, one on top of the other.

Say, "Look at and remember the last card you dealt." Suppose it is the 3 of clubs.

Then you say to Laura, "Now, please place the cards you dealt on top of the deck and hand the cards to Joey. When you do that, please tell him the number of cards you counted."

Say to Joey, "Will you now please count off the same number of cards and name the last card you come to." Suppose it is the king of hearts.

Ask Joey to read what you wrote on the slip of paper you handed him at the beginning. It will be the king of hearts.

Pick up the cards that Joey just dealt and place them on top of the deck. Ask Laura to read aloud what you have written on her slip of paper.

She will call out "sxaplt." It makes no sense.

"Oh, I forgot to tell you," you say. "That's a secret code. What it means is the 3 of clubs. Was that your card?"

Once again, you are right on.

How the trick is presented: After you have received the shuffled deck, spread the cards face up between your hands and say: "Good, they look well mixed."

At the same time, look at and remember the card on top of the deck (it is at the bottom when the cards are face up).

This will be the king of hearts (or whatever it actually is; we only say the king of hearts in our example), which you will write on the piece of paper you hand to Joey.

When you pick up the cards which Joey had dealt, take a peek at the bottom card as you are placing them on the deck. That will be the 3 of clubs (or whatever it actually is; this is just an example), which you will call out as the answer to the "secret code."

Shuffle It

What the audience sees: Have someone shuffle a deck of cards, then hand them to you. Say, "Let's make sure they're well mixed," and then shuffle them again.

Hand the cards back and say, "Please cut the deck approximately in half, take the top half and spread the cards face down on a table. I will do the same with the bottom half." Then do so.

"Now," you say, "slide out any card from your part of the deck, look at it, remember it. Now square up your cards into a pile and place your selected card on top of it. Cut the deck and complete the cut."

After this is done, do exactly the same thing with your half of the deck. Then say, "The card I looked at was (for example) the 5 of spades. What was the name of the card you chose?"

The spectator names the card chosen and then you say, "Here's where the magic begins. I will now cause my card, the 5 of spades, to fly invisibly to your cards and to join the card you just named."

Snap your finger over your cards, then spread them out, face up on the table. The 5 of spades has vanished! Then say, "Please spread your cards out, face up."

When this is done, there is the 5 of spades — and it is right next to the spectator's chosen card.

How the trick is presented: When you take the deck from the spectator, glimpse the bottom card and remember it. In this case, it would be the 5 of spades. When you shuffle the deck, do an ordinary overhand shuffle.

Keep shuffling until you have one card left in your right hand (if you're shuffling from the right to the left hand). This will be the bottom card, the 5 of spades. Then just drop it on top of the cards in your left hand.

Now the 5 of spades will be on top of the deck. When you take a card out from your half of the deck, simply pretend to look at it. It doesn't matter what it is, because you will call out the 5 of spades. But that card is really already on top of the spectator's cards!

The rest of this trick works automatically. It is a very easy trick, which is quite surprising. But practise the shuffling part well, It's useful for other card tricks too.

Red and Black

What the audience sees: From a deck of cards you deal off a number of cards and hand them to a spectator. "Please hold this packet of cards down behind your back," you say.

Then deal off a similar number of cards for yourself and place the balance of the deck aside. Hold your packet of cards behind your back also and say, "Now please mix your cards as much as you want but keep them face down. I will do the same."

After this is done, ask your assistant to remove any card from her packet and bring that selected card forward, still face down, so that no knows what it is. You do the same.

Now say, "Please give me your card and take mine. Now take my card behind your back, turn it over and insert it into the middle of your packet. Again, I will do the same with your card.

"All done? Now bring your packet forward as I am doing and spread out the cards."

To everyone's amazement, the two face-up cards will match. For example, if one card is a red 10 (hearts), the other will also be a red 10 (diamonds). But that isn't all. Have the rest of the cards turned over, They will all be black!

Preparation: Place all the black cards at the face of the deck. Place the two red 10s behind the thirteenth black card.

How the trick is presented: Remove the thirteen black cards from the face of the deck (don't count them out loud) and hand them to your assistant. Then remove the rest of the black cards for yourself (along with the red 10s, which will then be at the bottom of your packet.)

When you ask to have the cards mixed, do not actually mix yours but move your elbows a bit so that it looks as if you're mixing them. Hand the bottom 10 to your assistant.

Take her card and place it face down on top of your packet, then take your 10 from the bottom, turn it over, and insert it into the middle of your cards. The trick is done.

After the red cards are revealed, everyone will think it is over. Pretend that it is. Then say, "But wait, watch this." Wave your hands over the remaining cards and ask someone to turn them over — and watch the faces of your audience!

The Talking Deck

What the audience sees: Riffle-shuffle a deck of cards two or three times to show they are well mixed. To do this, cut the deck in half, place each half on a table with one half under your right hand and one under your left. Riffle the end of each pile with your thumbs, from the bottom up, and push the two piles together as you do so. This will reassemble the deck and mix the cards at the same time.

Now, spread the deck between your hands, face down, and have someone choose any card, look at it, remember it, and place it back in the deck. Place the deck on the table and say, "There is a magic card in this deck which will tell us where your card is located. Let me listen to it."

Put your ear to the cards, then say, "No, not a word. Let's have a look." Spread the cards, then suddenly in the middle of the deck, you will see one card face up. Let's say it is a 6. Say, "The magic card seems to be telling us something. Let's count down six cards below it." Have someone do so and turn over the sixth card. To everyone's surprise, it will be the chosen card.

Preparation: Take any card (in our example a 6 card), reverse it, and place it sixth from the bottom of the deck. If you choose a 4, place it fourth from the bottom and so on.

How the trick is presented: When you riffle-shuffle the deck, be sure to first drop a sufficient number of cards from the original bottom, so that when you weave the two halves together, you won't disturb the reversed card and the cards beneath it.

After the spectator has pulled out and noted the selected card, have her drop it on top of the deck. Then cut off about half the bottom of the deck and drop it on top. This will leave the card lost in the middle, but the reversed magic card will be in place above it. The rest is automatic but that's where you use your magical showmanship. Practise the riffle shuffle — it's very useful in many tricks.

Do as I Do

What the audience sees: Bring or borrow two decks of cards. Ask a spectator to assist you. Hand him one of the packs as you both sit down at a table. Tell him: "You must do everything as I do," as you begin shuffling your cards. If he doesn't begin to mix his cards, remind him, "Remember, do as I do." He will then shuffle his deck. You then say, "Let's change decks." After you have done so, place your deck face down in front of you, and wait for him to follow. Take a card from the middle of your pack, look at it, and place it face down on top of the pack. Direct him to do the same with his cards, but remind him to remember the card he pulled out.

Cut your deck and complete the cut. Then cut it a second and a third time. See that your assistant does the same. Then rotate your right hand over the cards in a mystical manner. Again he will mimic your motions. Then say, "Let's change decks again," and do so.

Now, direct your assistant, "Please look through your cards and remove the card you have chosen. Don't let me see it — place it face down on the table. I'll pull my chosen card out of these cards that I'm holding." After you have done this, place your card face down beside your assistant's chosen card.

At this point you will say, "So far you have followed my directions quite accurately. Let's see if you did so with the chosen cards. Please turn your card over." After he has done so, slowly turn yours over. The two cards will be exactly the same!

How the trick is presented: At the beginning, after you have both shuffled your cards and you are handing your deck to the assistant, tilt the cards slightly so that you can peek at the bottom card. Suppose it is the 5 of Clubs. Remember it. Then you do the Key card maneuver. When he cuts his cards and places the bottom half of the deck on top, the Key card (the 5 of Clubs) will be on top of his chosen card. No matter how many times he cuts after that, it will remain there, because the order of the cards does not change when you cut the deck.

When you select *your* chosen card, pretend to look at it and concentrate, but pay no attention to what it is — just remember that Key card. After you change decks the second time, just look for the 5 of Clubs. The selected card will be the one under it. Remove it and place it on the table. Of course, if the 5 of Clubs happens to be the bottom card, the selected one will be on top of the deck.

Meanwhile, your assistant will be pulling out the actual card that he chose, even though it is from another deck.

To make the trick more entertaining, you can add any gestures that you like, for your assistant to follow. You can stand up and sit down, touch the top of your head, or do anything that will get a chuckle from your audience. This very effective trick is one of the classical "oldies" of card magic, and it is so easy to do.

9
Money Tricks

Fantastic Fruit

What the audience sees: Have someone mark his initials on a dime so it can be identified later. Have him drop it into an envelope. Seal the envelope and place it on a table. Then show an orange, pick up a small knife, and slowly cut the orange in half. Just before it is sliced in two, pull the halves apart. Believe it or not, there will be a dime inside.

Ask the person who marked the coin to look at it. His initials will be right there on the dime. Is it the same dime that was dropped into the envelope? Tear up the envelope and toss the pieces into the air.

It is empty!

Preparation: Stick a tiny piece of soft soap to one side of the knife near the handle. It must be on the side facing you when you do the cutting. Place the knife in an envelope. Take another envelope and cut a small slit at one side of the bottom. Place both envelopes and an orange on the table before you begin the trick.

How the trick is presented: After the dime is dropped into the envelope with the hole in the bottom, hold your right hand under it and seal the envelope. Tilt the envelope so that the dime will drop through the slit into your right palm. Place the envelope on the table and, with your right hand, reach into the other envelope for the knife.

While your hand is in the envelope, stick the dime to the soapy surface on the knife. The envelope conceals what you are doing. Take out the knife and begin to cut the orange, making sure that the dime is not seen by the audience.

When you've cut more than halfway through, push the knife further forward so that the part with the coin enters the orange. Then just scrape the dime against the pulp. Separate the halves with your hands and show the dime. By tearing up the other envelope, you will destroy the evidence; the slit will not be noticed.

A terrific trick, but remember to practise all the moves ahead of time.

Quick Change

What the audience sees: Ask someone in your audience if they would lend you a quarter. Before it is handed to you, ask the person to mark her initials on the coin with a pen or pencil, so that they will recognize it later.

Drop the coin into an envelope. Seal the envelope and hold it up with your left hand.

With your right hand, reach into your pocket and remove a small change purse. Place it on a table top. Say, "This little purse has strange, magical qualities which I don't understand.

"It's really very valuable but if anything happens to your quarter in the envelope, you can have this little purse in exchange. Is that fair?"

Next, tear up the envelope into as many small pieces as you can, hold them high above the purse and then let them go so that the pieces of paper float down over the purse.

No quarter falls out, "Isn't that strange," you say. "The quarter seems to have vanished."

Next, ask the person who lent you the quarter to open the change purse. You guessed it — the marked quarter will be inside! "Whew," you say, "that's a relief! I can keep my magic purse!"

Preparation: Take a regular-sized mailing envelope and with a small pair of scissors cut a 5-centimeter (2-inch) slit in the right-hand bottom, near the corner (right means that when the

envelope's fold is facing you, the right corner is at your right hand.)
Place a small change purse in a right-hand pocket, leaving it
open with the mouth facing up.

How the trick is presented: After you have sealed the envelope
and you are holding it with the flap facing you, tilt it slightly
downwards at the right side, while holding it with both hands.
Your right hand should be positioned so that the palm is under
the right lower corner of the envelope.
The quarter will slide down and out through the slit, falling into
your right palm.
Bend your fingers to conceal it as you reach into your pocket.
Don't rush.
Drop the coin into the purse in your pocket and close the catch.
It's all done.
The rest is showmanship. Remember, when your tear up the
envelope, you are destroying the evidence of the secret opening.
Practise the moves with the envelope. It's easy!

Coin Slide

What the audience sees: Hold a small rectangle of cardboard
horizontally in your left hand. It should be about 8 centimeters
wide and 12 centimeters long (3 by 5 inches). Hold it between your
thumb and fingertips at one of the narrow ends.

Say, "If someone would be kind enough to place five pennies
on this little tray, I will show you how to make money vanish."

After the pennies are placed on the cardboard, ask someone to
cup their hands together, then tilt the "tray," pouring the pennies
into their hands. As you do so, say, "Close your hands quickly and
hold the pennies tightly. Now, when I say 'raeppasid' ('disappear'
backwards), you will feel the coins dissolve into nothingness."

After you say the magic word, say to your assistant, "Don't open
your hands, but tell us, have they gone?" The answer will of course
be "No." Then you say "All right, if we can't make them vanish then
let's make them multiply — let's double them.

"Are you ready? Ylpitlum elboud. Now, open your hands. There
now will be 10 pennies in your assistant's hands.

Preparation: Cut out two pieces of cardboard, exactly the same size, about 8 by 12 centimeters (3 by 5 inches). Paste them together this way: Apply paste to one piece along both long edges and one short edge. Fasten the other piece to it. Now, we have what looks like a piece of cardboard but what is actually a double piece with a secret pocket between the two — with a secret opening at one end. Drop 5 pennies into the secret pocket.

How the trick is presented: When you have the 5 pennies placed on the tray, you will be holding the end with the opening. Before you tilt the coins into the spectator's hands, transfer the tray to your right hand, holding it by the closed end.

Now, when you pour down the coins, the hidden pennies will slide out, joining the coins from the top. This will not be noticed if you hold the tray close to the assistant's hands and help her close them quickly with your left hand.

The trick is done.

The Weeping Coin

In the following trick I refer to the Queen, whose portrait appears on Canadian quarters. On the American quarter, of course, it will be George Washington who sheds the tears.

What the audience sees: Ask someone to lend you a quarter. Show the side that has an engraving of the Queen and say, "Some people think the Queen doesn't look too happy here. What do you think?"

After there have been some replies, say, "You may not believe it, but there have been times when she has been so sad I've actually seen her cry. You don't think so? Well, this just happens to be one of those times. Watch."

At this point, hold the coin in the fingertips of your right hand and rub it against your left elbow. Then hold it between the fingertips of both hands. All this time, it has been held with the Queen side facing you. Turn the coin around and the audience will see tears running down the Queen's face. Unbelievable.

Preparation: Dip a small piece of tissue paper into water. Squeeze it so that just a little excess water remains in it. Press it into a small pellet and hide it behind your left ear.

How the trick is presented: When you are rubbing the quarter against your left elbow, your left arm should be bent so that your hand is at your left ear. It is then easy to pick up the wet paper secretly and push it into the crook of your left thumb. After that, you are ready for the main move. When you are holding the coin between your hands — remember, the Queen is facing you — tilt your hands slightly downward. Then squeeze your left thumb against the index finger.

A little water will be forced out of the wet pellet, will run down the inside of the inside of the thumb and finger on to the Queen side of the coin and will drip off the coin. When you turn the quarter around, the "tears" will seem to be coming from the Queen.

The reason you should tilt your hands downward is so that the water will go in the right direction to hit the coin. Be sure to practise this well before you present it to your audience.

At the finish, reach into a left-hand pocket to remove a tissue to wipe the coin dry. Secretly drop the wet pellet into your pocket when you do this. Now you have nothing to hide.

Heads or Tails

What the audience sees: Place three coins on a table and ask someone to blindfold you. Then give the following instructions: "I would like someone to turn over any one of the coins, one at a time. You can turn over any particular coin, as many times as you like.

"You can turn over just as many coins as you wish. The only thing that I ask is that each time you turn over a coin, you call out the magic word 'supercalafragelisticexpialadosius.'

"When you wish to stop, place one hand over one of the coins and then remove my blindfold."

When all this has been done, turn to the table and say "I will use my X-ray glasses to look right through your hand."

Put on a pair of dark glasses and stare at the person's hand which covers the coin. Say, "Ah, I can see it quite clearly," and tell the audience whether heads or tails is up. You will always be right, no matter how many times the audience would like you to repeat the trick.

Preparation: Have three coins and a pair of sunglasses ready.

How the trick is presented: At the beginning, see how many heads are showing. If there are one or three, think "odd." If there are none or two, think "even." If you start with odd, keep thinking "odd" until the magic word is called out. Then switch to thinking "even."

So every time the coin is turned and the magic word is called out, you must switch your thinking back and forth from odd to even.

When your blindfold is removed just look at the two exposed coins. If there is one head — and you ended by thinking "odd" — the hidden coin will be a tail. If there are no heads showing, or two, the concealed coin will be a head.

If you ended on even, and there is one head showing, the concealed coin will be a head. An even number of heads means the concealed coin will be a tail.

Deceptive Dollars

What the audience sees: Show both your hands empty as you say, "How would you like to be a real magician and pull money from the air?" I don't want to brag, but I can do it anytime. And just to show there's nothing up my sleeves, I'll pull them up."

After you have done this, put your palms together and make a rubbing motion. To their astonishment, your audience will see several dollar bills emerge from between your clasped hands. "These are only $1 bills," you say then. "I haven't learned to produce $20s yet!"

Preparation: Place a few dollar bills one on top of the other, then roll them into a tight bundle. Tie the bundle together with a very thin thread which is easily breakable.

Now, tuck the roll of bills into the crook of your left elbow and pull some of your sleeve material back over it to conceal it. You should be wearing a jacket or a loose sweater. Remember to keep your left arm slightly bent as you begin the trick — just enough to so that the bills don't show or drop out.

How the trick is presented: When you offer to pull up your sleeves, first pull up your right sleeve, then the left. Grab the left sleeve just below the elbow and pull up. You'll find that your right hand passes right over the roll of bills.

Grip them together and keep them concealed in your half-closed hand as you clasp both hands together.

Then, as you start the rubbing motion with your hands, work your left hand thumb under the thread and break it. Then gradually push the bills out of your hands, one at a time, if you can. It looks better than just pushing out the whole bundle. A little practice will show you how easily this can be done.

I.O.U. $10

What the audience sees: Show both sides of a handkerchief and drop it on one side of a tabletop. Ask someone to lend you a ten-dollar bill. Crumple it up into a small ball and place it on the table. Take another handkerchief from your pocket and hand it to that person. As you pick up the crumpled bill with your right hand, say, "Would you please drape the hanky over my hand. Now, you can feel your ten under the hanky — hold on to it through the cloth." This will leave your assistant holding the bill with the hanky draped over it.

Reach into your right hand pocket and remove a book of matches. Light one of the matches and hold the flaming match close to the hanky, moving it slowly back and forth as you say, "Would you believe that this will cause your ten-dollar bill to vanish while you are holding it?"

Your assistant will say, "No, I can still feel it." Ask him to remove the hanky. This will reveal that he is now holding a crumpled piece of paper. When he opens it he will read the message "I.O.U. ten dollars." "Fair enough," you say, "give me the I.O.U and I'll return your ten." When he hands the paper to you, ask him to lift the first handkerchief you had dropped on the table. His bill will be under it.

Preparation: Crumple up a ten-dollar bill and place it, with a handkerchief, in a left-hand pocket. Cut out a piece of paper the same size as a bill and write the I.O.U message on it, then crumple it up. Place it in a right-hand pocket, along with another hanky and a book of matches.

How the trick is presented: When you pull out the first hanky with your left hand, conceal the crumpled ten under your last three fingers, which are bend around the bill. You will be gripping the hanky by the thumb and forefinger. Use your right hand to open the hanky and show both sides. As you casually place the opened hanky on the table, secretly drop the bill under it.

When you remove the second hanky from your right-hand pocket, palm the crumpled paper in the same manner with your right hand fingers. After you pick up your assistant's bill, and the hanky is draped over it, it's easy to switch the paper ball for the bill under cover of the hanky.

After the assistant takes hold of the hanky and paper ball, reach your right hand into your pocket for the matches, at the same time leaving the concealed ten there. The trick is done. The rest is pure showmanship.

Remember to practise the switching of the paper and bill, and the palming of the small balls. This "finger palm" is very useful in many tricks with small objects — particularly with coins.

The Wandering Coin

What the audience sees: Borrow a quarter from someone and have it marked for identification. Toss it from your right hand into your left hand, which closes into a fist as you say, "I should have a magic wand somewhere," and reach into your inside left-hand jacket pocket with your right hand. Pull out a pencil with the remark, "I know what you're thinking, but this really *is* a magic wand in disguise. Now watch what happens."

Wave the pencil over your left fist. Slowly open your left hand to show the coin has vanished. Also show your right hand to be empty.

Now say, "That was my vanishing wand. Now I need my reproduction wand." Remove another pencil from your pocket with your right hand. Show your clenched left fist again, wave the pencil over it, and slowly open your left hand. The quarter will reappear! Have it examined to prove it is the original coin.

Preparation: Place a couple of pencils in your left-hand inside jacket pocket.

How the trick is presented: When you borrow the marked quarter be sure to receive it in your right hand. Let it slide into the "finger palm" position, at the base of the last three fingers of your hand (the middle finger, the ring finger, and the pinky). When you bend these fingers to your palm the coin will be retained and concealed beneath them.

Bring your right hand toward your left, which is held palm up. Touch the left side of your right hand to the right side of the left as you tilt the right hand to apparently slide the coin into the left palm. As you do so, bend the right fingers to palm the coin, and close the left fist as you draw it away. This move is called the "pass," and is an important and useful move in sleight-of-hand. The effect will be that you have tossed the coin into your left hand.

Now, when you reach inside your jacket to get the pencil, first drop the coin into your left sleeve at the armhole, while keeping your left arm bent at the elbow. The coin will fall down as far as your elbow and remain there.

When you are ready to reproduce the coin with the second "wand," as you reach with your right hand for the pencil, lower your left arm and raise the fingers of your left hand to catch the coin as it falls. Then close your left fist. You are now ready for the climax.

The time you spend practising the pass will be time well spent. There are many different methods of doing it. This is one of the simplest and least suspicious-looking ways — if it is done properly. The timing of your moves is important. You will feel awkward at first, but smoothness and confidence will come with practice. The move involving the jacket sleeve will be another useful sleight in your repertoire.

This is one of those beautiful little tricks that take but a few moments, but can be done impromptu, anywhere, and make a strong impression on your audience.

10
Mental Tricks

Incredible

This trick is sold on the magic market in various forms. However, it is in the public domain. Use it — and mystify your friends.

What the audience sees: Write something on a piece of paper, fold it, and hand it to someone to hold. Then deal six playing cards in a row on the table. The first card will be face down the second face up, the third face down, the fourth face up, the fifth face down, and the sixth face up.

Say to the person who is holding the paper, "As you can see, we have six cards here. I want you to think of any number from 1 to 6. Have you decided on the number? Would you like to change your mind?

"All right, would you please call out the number you have chosen."

Whatever the number called out, count the cards from one end of the row. When the card is selected, ask the person, "Would you please read the prediction on the piece of paper you are holding?"

You will have predicted the actual card chosen.

Preparation: Have the following six cards ready on top of the deck: 3 of clubs, ace of clubs, 6 of diamonds, 4 of spades, 9 of clubs, 8 of spades. The ace should be the only card with a different-colored back. You must use a blue-backed deck, with the ace taken from a red-backed deck.

How the trick is presented: Lay out the cards from left to right: the 3 face down, the ace face up (make sure the red back is not shown), the 6 face down, the 4 face up, the 9 face down, the 8 face up.

On the paper, write "I predict you will choose the only red card."

Now, here's what you have to do. If the number 1 is called out, say, "1? You have selected the ace."

Turn all the cards face down. The ace is the only red card. Right on.

Number 2? Count the cards from left to right, "1, 2." Again the ace.

Number 3? Count again from left to right. You get the red 6. Turn over the face-down cards to show it is the only red card.

Number 4? Count from right to left this time. The 6 again.

Number 5? Count from right to left again. The ace again.

Number 6? Say, "You have chosen the 6" as you turn it over.

So you can see, you can't lose — no matter which number is chosen. I predict that this effect will become one of your favorites.

Silent Spell

What the audience sees: Lay down 10 different objects on a table top and spread them around. Ask for a volunteer and say, "We haven't spoken about this before, have we? All right, I would like you to think of just one of these objects. I am going to touch each one in turn. As I do so, please spell out silently the object you are thinking of, one letter for each tap.

"When you come to the last letter, please ask me to stop."

When you are asked to stop, you ask your volunteer: "What were you thinking of?" Your finger will be on it. It always works!

Preparation: Have the following items ready: key, fork, watch, pencil, pair of glasses, notebook, paper clip, half-dollar, thermometer, and handkerchief. If you look at each item in turn, you will see that the first, key, has three letters, the second has four (fork), the third has five (watch) and so on.

How the trick is presented: When you begin tapping the objects, you can touch any 2 for the first two taps.

Then touch the key, then the fork, then each object in the order of the number of letters it contains. When you are asked to stop, you automatically will be on the chosen object.

You will have to memorize the order of the objects that you touch. This is the only thing that you need to practise.

Be sure that you do not lay out the objects themselves in the order of spelling. That might be a giveaway.

But you could lay them out in a certain arrangement that would make it easy for you to remember the order in which to tap them.

Also, you do not have to use the objects named above. You may use anything handy, as long as it has the number of letters you require for that object.

When you tap each object, take your time. Make it look as though you are thinking and trying to read the spectator's mind.

Mathematical Matches

What the audience sees: Hand a full matchbook to a spectator and say, "Please turn around so that I can't see what you're doing. Tear out as many matches as you wish and place them in your pocket. Have you done so? Now count how many matches are left in the matchbook and add the digits of that total.

"For example, if there are 12 matches, add the 1 and the 2 to get 3. Whatever your total is, remove that number of matches from the matchbook and place them in your pocket along with the others."

When all this has been done, give these final instructions: "Now just tear out a few more matches and keep them in your hand. Hand me the matchbook, please."

When this is done, ask the spectator to count the matches in his hand and to concentrate on that number. You say, "Believe it or not, I will now tell you the number of matches you are holding in your hand. Remember, there is no possible way I can tell how many matches you have removed."

After a few moments of deep concentration say, "I believe I have received the message," and call out a number. You will be correct.

Preparation: Be sure to use a regular-size matchbook, not an extra-large one. The regular ones always contain 20 matches. Many people are not aware of this. Also be sure that no matches have been removed previously from the book.

How the trick is presented: When the spectator finally hands the matchbook back to you, it will be open. If it is not, simply flip it open with your thumb as you are talking to the audience.

All you have to do is casually glance at the matches and make a mental note of how many are left. Subtract this number from 9 — and that will be the number in the spectator's hand. If the earlier instructions are followed correctly, there will always be 9 matches left in the matchbook, before the last batch is removed. All you have to do is a simple subtraction. What could be easier? Yet the trick is very mystifying.

Think-A-Date

What the audience sees: Tear several pages out of a calendar which you do not need, each page, of course, being one month of the year. Spread these out on a table and ask someone to mentally choose one of those months, but not to disclose which one it is. Then turn over each page, leaving them all, face down, spread around the table top.

Now, say to the person who selected the month, "I'm going to touch some of the pages, one at a time. When I begin, please spell out the letters of your chosen month mentally, as I touch each page. When you come to the last letter, say 'stop' out loud."

When this is done and the spectator calls out "stop," say, "Will you please tell us what month you mentally selected." After the month is named, turn over the last page you had touched. It will be the chosen month.

How the trick is presented: Tear out seven pages from a calender, preferably an old one from the previous year. Be sure to tear out the following months in this order: May, June, April, August, October, November, September. Do you notice anything interesting about those chosen months? Of course. Starting with May, which has three letters, each month has one more letter than the one that comes before it.

When you place them on the table, spread them in some kind of pattern, so that you will remember their positions. Think of May as number 3, June as number 4, April as number 5 and so on. When you begin touching the pages, touch any two pages to start off. Then touch number 3, which is May, then number 4, June, and continue touching each page in its proper order.

Keep going until you are told to stop. You can see how it works out — you can't miss. If someone asks you to repeat the trick, say "I'll make it more difficult by using some other months."

Substitute December for November, January for October, July for June, and March for April. As you can see, the number of letters for these substitutions is the same. The only thing you really have to practise for this clever trick is laying out the pages in an order you will remember, but not in a straight line.

Matchup

What the audience sees: Open a brown paper bag and stand it on a table top. Hand out several slips of paper to several members of your audience. Ask each person to write a 3-digit number on the paper and then drop it into the bag. After this is done, lift up the bag above eye level and ask someone to mix the slips. Then reach inside, and without looking into the bag, take out one slip, hand it to someone to whom you have previously given an extra slip of blank paper and say, "Please write down the numbers on this paper."

Then you say, "It is possible I might have seen those numbers, so here are some more slips of paper. Would some of you take these and write down some more 3-digit numbers. Now, before you drop them into the bag, fold the papers into quarters so that the numbers will be hidden."

After all this is done, reach into the bag again, remove a folded slip, and hand it to the same person as before. "Would you please write down the numbers on this piece of paper under the other numbers you wrote down?" you say. "Now, to keep you really busy, I'd like you to multiply the two sets of numbers together."

While the spectator is doing this, jot something down on a piece of paper, tear it off, and hand it to someone. When the multiplication is completed, ask for the answer to be called out. Then ask for the numbers on your torn piece to be called out. Believe it or not — they will be the same.

Preparation: Write the number 143 on one of your slips, fold it in quarters and fasten it a few inches above the bottom of the bag, on the inside, with a tiny piece of adhesive tape.

How the trick is presented: When you remove the first slip of paper, peek at the numbers on it and remember them. When you reach in the second time, remove your hidden slip. What you finally jot down is this: Suppose the first number is 652. Write it down twice, like this: 652, 652 (in your case, whatever the first number was). Then divide it by 7. Write down the answer, tear it off, and hand it to someone.

The two totals will always match.

Super Prediction

What the audience sees: Remove an envelope from your pocket, and from it remove three crayons — a red, blue, and a green. Place the envelope aside on the table and lay out the three crayons side by side. Say, "Now, I would like you to select one of these crayons. You may not believe it, but I will mentally influence your choice. Please tune in to my thought waves and then select the color you wish — I should say the color I wish. I have already written my prediction. We'll get to that in a moment." When someone selects one of the crayons, you immediately show your prediction. It will be right on.

Preparation: On a piece of paper write "You will select red." Place the paper inside an envelope with the three crayons. On the face of the envelope write "You will select blue." On the paper wrapping of the green crayon, along one side, write "This is the one."

How the trick is presented: When removing the crayons from the envelope, be sure to hold the face toward you, so that the writing is not seen. When you lay the envelope down on the table, lay it on its face — again so that the writing will not be seen. When you put the crayons down, be sure to put the green one down so that the writing is at the bottom and is not revealed. If the red crayon is selected, pick up the envelope, keeping the face toward you, remove the paper from inside and show it. If the blue crayon is chosen, just turn over the envelope and show the prediction written on the face. If the green crayon is picked, ask the person to pick it up and read the prediction on it. So in every case you will be right. You just can't lose. End up by placing the crayons back in the envelope and dropping it into your pocket. Of course, this is one trick you cannot repeat for the same audience.

Sensitive Fingertips

Here is a great mind-reading effect which really fools people but is so easy to do.

What the audience sees: Ask someone in the audience to act as a subject, so that you can read her mind. Let us suppose her name is Laura. Say, "I am going out of the room. After I leave, will you all decide on a number, say between 1 and 25, and will you tell it to Laura? Then call me back in."

After all this is done, and you re-enter the room, look very serious and say, "Now, Laura, I am going to try to read your mind and tell you the number that was chosen when I was out of the room.

"Would you sit on this chair in the middle of the room, and I will stand behind you."

Place the fingertips of each hand on Laura's temples and say, "I am going to call out different numbers. When I call out the chosen number, please think 'That's it! That's it!' With my super-sensitive fingertips, I will try to pick up your brainwaves.

"Don't say a word or make a move. I will get the message."

Then begin to count, "One, two, three..." When you come to the chosen number, you will stop and say, "I seem to feel those waves. Yes, they're coming through." Then repeat the chosen number. You will be right!

Preparation: Laura is your secret assistant. And you just have to teach her one thing: to press her teeth together tightly.

How the trick is presented: When you count off the numbers, Laura is waiting to hear the chosen number. As soon as you call it, all she has to do is press her teeth tightly together. Try this while you hold your fingertips to your temple. You'll feel an outward pressure that's easy to notice.

So as Laura clenches her teeth, you will immediately know the chosen number. Your sensitive fingertips are certainly feeling something — but it's not brainwaves.

It's a good idea to have someone blindfold you before you re-enter the room. The whole thing will seem more mysterious.

Telephone Telepathy

What the audience sees: Ask someone to think of any three-digit number (three different digits) and to write down. Suppose it is 526. Ask her to reverse the number (to 625) and to subtract the lesser number from the greater. This would be 625 minus 526 equals 99.

Ask your assistant if her subtraction yields 2 or 3 digits. If two (as in 99), ask her to place a zero at the beginning, giving 099.

Now say "Please add this number to the reverse of it." Thus she would do the following: 099 plus 990 equals 1089.

Then ask her how many digits she now has. She will say 4.

"All right," you reply, "please read out your total."

When the number is called out, hand her a telephone book and say: "Your total is 1089. Would you like to choose the tenth name on page 89 or the 89th name on page 10? It is your choice."

Whichever she chooses, ask her to turn to that page and look up the location at that location.

"Please concentrate on the name, address, and phone number. I will try to read your thoughts," you tell her.

Then you write something on the page of a notepad, tear it off, and hand it to a third person. Ask the other person to now read out from the telephone book the name, address, and telephone number. Then ask the person holding the scrap of paper to read out what you have written.

To everyone's astonishment, it will be exactly the same!

Preparation: Have a telephone book, a notepad, and a pencil ready. Look up the name, address, and phone number on page 10, line 89 of the phone book. Write it down on the first page of the notepad. Do the same for page 89, line 10. Your numerical instructions will always end up with the total 1089, of course.

How the trick is presented: When performing this trick, hold the pad so that no one will notice the writing on the first page. When the choice of page is made, look at your notes, pretend to write something, tear off the page, crumple it up and place it in your pocket, saying: "No, that's wrong. I'll try again."

Then write the correct message, which you just memorized, on the next page.

Mental Vision

This is a trick using playing cards, but it should be presented as a mind-reading effect, not as a card trick.

What the audience sees: Ask any member of the audience to come forward. Make it clear that this is to be a volunteer and that there has been no previous collusion between the two of you. Show a deck of cards which you are holding face down. Say to your assistant, "I'd like you to face the audience and hold this deck face down behind your back. Then, would you please cut off a portion of the top part of the deck, reverse it so that it is now face up, and place it underneath the rest of the deck." As you are saying this, demonstrate what she is to do. After she does this, say, "All right, please bring the deck forward. Now you have two halves of the deck face to face. If you look through it you will come to two cards that are actually touching face to face. You could have cut the deck at any place — so there is no way that you or I or anyone here can know what those two cards are. Right?"

Turn your back and say, "Will you please look through the cards until you locate those two cards. You have them? All right, now show them to the audience and remember them. Now put them back in the deck so that I can't see them when I turn back."

At this point you go into your mind-reading demonstration. Ask the assistant to visualize the two cards while you go into a deep concentration. After a minute or two, name one of the cards, and then the other. You will be correct on both counts.

Preparation: Look at the bottom card of the deck and memorize it. Take any other card, remember it too, and place it face *up*, under the bottom card.

How the trick is presented: As you can see, no matter where the deck is cut, when the reversed top half is placed under the bottom half, the same two cards (which you memorized) will always be facing each other. You can't lose.

It is important to demonstrate clearly to the assistant what she is to do behind her back, because if she doesn't follow instructions the whole thing will be ruined. When you are showing her how to cut and reverse the cards, do not actually place the cut-off section under the rest of the cards. Just make it clear to your assistant how she should handle the cards.

It's easy to set up the deck beforehand, even when you are in front of the audience. After you have done a card trick or two, simply fiddle around with the cards a bit, secretly place the reversed card, and put the deck down, ignoring it for a few minutes.

The impact of this effect depends mainly on how you act out the "mind-reading" portion. Don't be afraid to ham it up.

11
Miscellaneous Tricks

Rattle Boxes

This trick is a classic. It has been around for many years.

What the audience sees: Place three small penny matchboxes on a table top and say, "I'd like to see how observant you can be. I have three matchboxes here. One contains some matches, the other two are empty. Here, I'll show you."

Shake each box in turn. Everyone will hear the matches rattling in one box. There will be no sound from the other two. "Now," you say, "I'm going to move the boxes around. Let's see if you can follow the full one."

You then proceed to slowly slide the boxes into different positions on the table. Ask someone to point out the one he thinks contains the matches. Pick up the one he chooses and shake it. He will be correct.

"Perhaps if I do it a little faster, you'll find it a little more difficult."

You move the boxes around again, this time a little faster. "Now where is it?" you ask. This time, when the guess is made, the spectator will be wrong. The chosen box will be wrong. The chosen box will not rattle but one of the other boxes will.

Continue this procedure several times. The spectators will always miss.

The last time you do it, they will guess right. Then you say, "Well, of course, how could you be wrong? *All* the boxes are full!"

Then you pick up the remaining two boxes in turn and shake them. They will all rattle.

Preparation: Buy four matchboxes, They are available at most variety stores. Empty three of them and tape the ends so that they cannot be opened.

Remove about half the matches from the fourth box, then close it. Tape this box to the underside of your forearm, near the wrist, but hidden by your sleeve.

How the trick is presented: Whenever you want to shake a box to show it is empty, simply pick it up with your left hand and shake it. If you wish to show that it is full, pick it up with your right hand.

Your audience will hear the hidden box rattle but the sound will seem to be coming from the box you are holding. You can then be in control of whether the box you show will be empty or full.

The first time you move the boxes, let the spectator be correct. He will then think it is easy and will be most surprised later, when he is proved wrong.

The last time, pick each of them up with your right hand. Your audience will think all the boxes are full. It makes for a knockout ending to an excellent trick.

A Surprising Straw

This is an entertaining trick that ends with a big laugh.

What the audience sees: Hold a handkerchief by the middle of one side in your left hand. Show a small drinking straw, held at one end, in your right hand. Hold the straw vertically and drape the hanky over it. Your audience will see the outline of the straw holding up the center of the hanky. Your right hand, with the straw, will be covered by the hanky.

Now slowly raise your right hand in front of your face. Grasp the center of the hanky with your left hand and whip it away.

The straw will be gone! All your audience sees is the palm of your right hand facing them — and it is empty. Say, "How's that," and you'll be sure to get applause.

Then wait a moment and slowly move your hand away from in front of your face — and your audience will burst out laughing. Because there is the straw, sticking out from between your clenched teeth!

Preparation: Get a regular plastic straw and cut it in half.

How the trick is presented: Hold the straw at one end between the tips of your right thumb and second finger. As soon as you cover your right hand with the hanky, extend your index finger vertically. At the same time, tilt your hand toward you by bending your wrist slightly, so that the straw is now almost horizontal and pointing toward you.

As you pull the hanky down over your hand, from front to back, drape it so that the straw is protruding from under the rear edge of the hanky. It will not be seen, because it is away from the audience and should be held close to your body.

The audience will see the center of the hanky being held up by what they think is the straw but what really is your finger. Now raise your hand in front of your face and grasp the straw between your teeth. Turn your hand so that the palm is facing out.

As you pull the hanky away, extend all your fingers — so that you are showing your hand empty. At the same time, your hand is hiding the straw. After the first surprise slowly move your hand to the side. The audience will find it really funny to see the straw sticking out of your mouth.

Matchbox Mystery

What the audience sees: Place a piece of newspaper or wrapping paper, or a sheet of writing paper, on a table top. Lay a penny, a nickel, and a quarter in a row on the paper. Take three penny matchboxes, empty out the matches, and pull out the drawers. Turn over a drawer on top of each of the coins. Now tell your audience, "I'm going to turn my back. Will someone remove any one of the coins and place it in a pocket. Then put the match drawer back where it was."

After this, say, "Please be quiet while I concentrate." Touch the top of each drawer, then do it again. Say, "Are you sure a coin was removed? I don't feel the vibrations." Repeat the touching routine, then stop with your finger on one of the covers. Say, "This seems to be the one. Someone has removed the quarter, right?" Yes, you are!

Preparation: Buy three penny matchboxes. Use any coins you like, or buttons, peanuts, etc.

How the trick is presented: The reason for placing the items on a sheet of paper is in order to have a soft surface. Because, when you place a drawer over each coin, you must hold the drawer with the middle finger in front and the thumb at the rear. And when you place the drawer down, you must press the tip of your thumbnail into the paper.

This will leave a mark behind each drawer — and each mark will be the same distance away from the back of the drawer. When a particular drawer is lifted to remove a coin, it will never be placed back in exactly the right spot.

So when you turn to look at the covers, you will know right away which cover has been moved. But don't point it out right away: make it seem that you are having a difficult time finding the missing coin.

This is a trick you can repeat!

Confetti Shower

What the audience sees: Show a sheet of tissue paper and tear it into small pieces. Bunch the pieces together into a little bundle, hold the bundle in your left fingertips, and dip it into a glass of water. Squeeze out the excess water and place the wet bundle into your right hand as you pick up a small paper fan with your left hand.

As you open the fan over your right hand, say, "We usually throw confetti at a wedding and we also have a shower for the bride beforehand — but have you ever heard of a shower of confetti?"

As you are saying this and waving the fan, a beautiful shower of confetti will fly out from your hand and fill the air.

Preparation: At a stationery or novelty store, buy a few sheets of colored tissue paper (all the same color) and a small paper fan. This should not cost more than a few cents.

With a pair of scissors, cut up some of the paper into tiny pieces like confetti.

Place these in the center of one of the sheets and bring up the sides, forming a small bag. Twist and tape it into a small bundle, then cut away the surplus paper.

You'll be left with a small, enclosed package of confetti. Have a glass of water standing on a table. Place the fan in a left-hand pocket.

How the trick is presented: Conceal the confetti package in your right hand when you are ready to begin. When you pretend to place the wet bundle into your right hand, you actually keep it hidden in your left.

This is easy. Practise it in front of a mirror so that you get it right. Then when your reach into your pocket for the fan — with your left hand — just drop the bundle into your pocket before you pull out the fan.

As you open the fan, dig your right thumbnail into the package in your right hand. This will tear the wrapping and release the confetti.

But keep your hand closed so that the confetti doesn't spill out. Then open your hand as you wave the fan over it.

The shower of confetti, which everyone expects to be a wet mass, is very showy. it is a real surprise too!

The Pencil Grows

What the audience sees: Show a pencil which is about 7 to 10 centimeters long (3 or 4 inches) and drop it into the top of your right coatsleeve. Of course it will drop down the sleeve and into your right hand if you lower your arm and curl your fingers up. Have someone make a mark on the pencil so that it can be identified later.

Then drop it into your right sleeve again. This time, it doesn't appear in your hand.

Say, "I wonder where it is?" then look toward your left hand. The pencil will now be there and it will be the same pencil, as the mark will show.

Then say, "I wonder what will happen if I drop it into my left sleeve" as you do so.

The audience will see it emerging from the bottom of your left sleeve, but as it emerges, it will seem to be getting longer and longer, until, when it is completely out, it is seen to be almost twice as long as it originally. A very surprising illusion!

Preparation: Get two identical pencils. Cut one in half. Sharpen both of them. Drop the large pencil down your left sleeve before you perform, but keep your elbow bent. This will keep the pencil from dropping any farther down your sleeve. You are ready to start.

How the trick is presented: After the pencil drops out of your right sleeve the first time, take it in your left hand. The second time, as you pretend to drop it into your sleeve, conceal it in your left hand, drop that hand to your side as you shake your right arm, and everyone will expect the pencil to drop out of your right sleeve.

The third time, take a pencil in your right hand and when you are pretending to drop it into your left sleeve, simply drop it into your left inside jacket pocket or a shirt pocket.

This is easy, because your jacket will be hiding your moves. As you lower your left arm, cup your left fingers so that they catch the long pencil, then gradually lower them so that the pencil emerges slowly. It seems to grow longer as it appears.

Picking Toothpicks

What the audience sees: Place a small box of toothpicks on a table and remove a bunch of them. Ask someone to do the same, saying, "Take as many as you wish, but not all of them. Don't let me see how many you have."

Quietly count your toothpicks to yourself, without revealing how many you have. Give the spectator two of your toothpicks and say: "If I give you two toothpicks, then I'll have as many as you, plus enough more to add up to 14.

"Now, please add up your toothpicks. How many do you have?" Suppose he says 7. Count off 7 of your own toothpicks, then count out the rest of them aloud:... 8, 9, 10, 11, 12, 13, 14 — right on, the number you predicted.

Before anyone can try to figure out how this works, say, "All right, I'll try to do this again." Repeat all the moves and again your prediction will be correct, even though it is not the same one.

Now quickly put away the toothpicks and start on another trick.

How the trick is presented: When you remove some toothpicks from the box, be sure that you take a little more than half the amount, so that the spectator can't have more than you.

Now, suppose you have 32 toothpicks. You give 2 to the spectator, which leaves you with 30 toothpicks. The statement that you now make is important: "If I give you two toothpicks, then I will have as many as you, plus enough more to add up to 30."

Suppose the spectator has 20 toothpicks. Count off your 20 toothpicks, along with the spectator, then continue with 21, 22, etc., until you reach your last toothpick, which is 30.

Isn't that amazing? Now you may be thinking, what is the secret? Well, that's the strange part — there is none. You're not making a prediction at all. You are actually just stating how many toothpicks you have. But nobody will realize that.

The reason I suggest going on to another trick right away is so that nobody will have time to think it over.

Penetrating a Table

What the audience sees: You are seated at the dinner table. Each person has a regular table setting, including a cloth napkin, spoon, knife, and fork.

Pick up your napkin in your right hand and say, "I'd like to show you a fantastic magic trick. Watch this carefully."

Raise your left hand so that your arm is vertical. Drape the napkin over your left hand so that it hangs down over the sleeve of your left arm.

With your right hand now free, pick up the spoon beside your bowl and slip it under the napkin between your left hand and yourself, the handle part upwards. The audience should be able to see the outline of the top of the handle protruding at the peak of the napkin.

Now, with your right thumb and first two fingers, grasp the point of the top of the handle through the napkin and lift the whole thing away from your left hand. Hold the napkin above the table and say, "Now, watch and listen."

Give the napkin a shake. Suddenly, everyone will hear the sound of something hitting the floor under the table. Toss the napkin in the air. The spoon has vanished. Have someone reach under the table. The spoon will be there.

Preparation: You should have a good-sized napkin and you must wear a jacket.

How the trick is presented: As soon as you place the spoon under the napkin, stretch your left index finger upwards. It will raise the napkin and make it appear that the tip of the spoon is there.

Slip the spoon itself into your left sleeve. It will drop down to your elbow. When you remove the napkin with your right hand, quickly bring your left index finger down. Everyone will think you are now holding the tip of the spoon handle through the napkin.

At this point, place your left arm on your left knee as you lean forward. As soon as you shake the napkin, tilt your left hand downward. The spoon will slip out of your sleeve and fall to the floor under the table.

The trick is done. Remember to practise this several times for smoothness and for proper timing.

Dice Deceptions

What the audience sees: Have three dice on a table top. Turn your back and ask someone to pick up the dice, shake them in her hand then, place them in a pile on the table, one on top of the other.

Turn back and say, "You can see that I have no idea what numbers are on the tops and bottoms of these dice, except, of course, the top die. Now, by pressing down on the top die, I will be able to tell you the total to which all the hidden faces add up."

Hold your forefinger on the top die for a minute or two, then announce the total. Have the dice checked. You will be right on.

Next, turn your back again and ask someone else to roll two of the dice, to add the total of the numbers which come up, then to turn over one of the dice and add the number now showing to the previous total."

Then say, "Now roll the die you just turned over and add the number which comes up to your total. Please write down your grand total."

Turn around and immediately announce the number just written. Everyone will be amazed.

How the trick is presented: Many people are not aware that the opposite sides of a die always add up to seven. So in the first part of this trick, the tops and bottoms of the three dice must add up to 21. When you turn back, you spot the number on top of the top die, deduct that from 21 and you automatically know the secret total.

When you are touching the top die, be sure to concentrate, to make it look more magical when you call out the number. Then go right on the the next part of the trick, so the audience won't have a chance to figure out what you did, even if they know about the opposite sides totalling seven.

For the second part, suppose the spectator rolls six and three, totaling nine. He turns over the three die, getting a four. His total is now 13. He rolls that die and gets a five. The grand total is 18.

You turn back and spot the two dice, which show a six and a five, adding up to 11. Add number seven, which gives you 18 — the secret number.

That's all you have to do each time you do this trick — add the number seven.

Calendar

What the audience sees: Hand someone a calendar of the year and ask them to select any month, without telling you which one.

Then ask, "What is your favorite day of the week? Is it Monday, because it means going back to work? Or maybe it is Saturday, because you can sleep in? Or maybe it's Sunday."

Suppose the answer is Tuesday. Then say, "Please choose any three consecutive Tuesdays in that month. Circle them with this pencil. Now add together the dates and call out your total."

As soon as this has been done, you will announce the three dates that were chosen. And you will be correct.

Then you ask another person to choose another month and you repeat the feat!

Preparation: Have a calendar of the year and a pencil handy.

How the trick is presented: After the total has been called out, all you have to do is mentally divide it by 3. The answer you get will be the middle date of the three which have been selected. Next, deduct 7 from that number and you will have the first date. Add 7 to that middle number and you will have the third date. That's all there is to it!

After you have repeated the trick with another month, say "I will now attempt something more difficult. Select yet another month, don't tell me what day you are choosing, but circle any four dates in a vertical column of that month.

"Please call out the total of those numbers."

You will immediately tell the audience what the dates are.

This is done a little differently. Subtract 14 from the total called out and then divide the result by 4. The answer you get will be the second date chosen. Subtract 7 to get the first date. Add 7 to get the third date. Add another 7 to get the last date chosen.

You can use a paper and pencil to do these calculations if you wish: it will not detract from the mystery of the presentation.

What's in a Name

Here's a new twist on another oldie.

What the audience sees: Ask each person in the audience to call out his or her first name in turn. If there are more than 10 people, just ask 10 to do so. As each name is called, write it on a separate, small piece of paper. When finished, fold each paper into a small packet, then drop then all into a bowl. Mix them well, then say: "Will someone choose one of these slips? Now open it and look at the name. Remember it but don't let me see it. Now place it in this ashtray. Here are some matches — please light the match and burn the paper."

After this is done, roll up your left sleeve and say: "What was the name on the paper you chose?" When the name is called out, say: "Please take the magic ashes from the ashtray and rub them right here on my arm."

To everyone's amazement, the chosen name will mysteriously appear, written on your arm.

Preparation: With a thin piece of soap, write on your forearm the name of a person you know will be there.

How the trick is presented: When the various people are calling out their names, repeat each name as you write, as if you are actually writing down that name — but each time, write the same name as the one you have written on your arm. Occasionally, you should ask how a name is spelled, to make it seem that you are actually writing down that name. If a name is long, take a little longer to write it. As you can see, you can't go wrong. No matter which slip is chosen, the spectator will get the name that's been prepared.

When the ashes are rubbed on your arm, make sure that enough of them are applied and that they are rubbed over the exact area where the name is written in soap.

Also, while the person is burning the paper, remove the remaining slips from the bowl and casually drop them in your pocket — thereby removing the evidence of your hanky panky.

The Magic Square

The is a trick using cards, but it is not really a card trick.

What the audience sees: Riffle-shuffle a deck of cards and place it face down on a table top. Ask someone to cut off approximately half the deck and place it down beside the bottom half. Pick up the bottom half and place it crosswise over the other cards, saying, "We'll just mark where you cut the deck." Take a paper and pencil and draw a square, marking off 25 areas, as shown in illustration A.

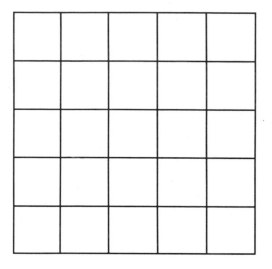

A

Then return to the cards, remove the top pack which is lying crosswise, and remove the two cards at the top of the bottom half, saying, "I'm going to place the top two cards that you cut to over here" — and lay them face down to one side, without showing their faces.

Now ask someone to write any number between 1 and 25 in any one of the blank squares. After this is done, randomly fill in every other square with numbers until every number from 1 to 25 has been inscribed. This is shown in illustration B.

12	25	8	16	4
18	1	14	22	10
24	7	20	3	11
5	13	21	9	17
6	19	2	15	23

B

At this point hand the pencil to a spectator and say, "Please add the numbers of each column separately, and mark the sum at the bottom of each." Each column will total 65! Ask someone else to add each row across. Again, 65! Ask another person to add both diagonal rows. You guessed it — 65!

By this time most people will have forgotten about the cards. Point to the two cards you had set aside, and say, "Now, isn't this a coincidence." Pick up one in each hand and slowly turn the faces to the audience. A 6 in your right hand, a 5 in your left!

Preparation: Place a 5 of any suit on top of a deck of cards, and a 6 on top of it.

How the trick is presented: When you interweave the two halves of the pack when riffle-shuffling them, be sure to retain the top few cards so that they fall on top when the shuffle is completed, so your 6 and 5 are undisturbed. After the deck is cut, and you place the bottom half crosswise over the other half, you are not marking the place where the deck was cut, as the spectators believe. You are actually marking the *top* of the deck, thereby "forcing" the choice of the cards you wish to be selected.

At that point you produce the paper and pencil to distract attention from your hanky panky with the cards — and then return to the deck to remove the two "selected" pasteboards.

Now we come to the mathematical part. What you see in illustration B is called a Magic Square. There is a system involved in creating it. Please follow the numbers as I describe it.

Suppose the assistant started with the number 7, and placed it in the square where it appears in the illustration. You must now begin entering consecutive numbers in order, until you reach 25, and then begin again with number 1 — thus filling every square. The system is this: when you wish to enter the 8, use the Knight's Move in chess. Mentally count two spaces up and one space to the right. As you see, that's where the 8 is located. Now, in order to place the 9, you can't go any farther up, so you start at the bottom of the row. Again, two up and one to the right. And there's the 9. The 10 follows in the same way. But look where the 11 is. The reason for that is, when you come to a multiple of 5, you use a different move — one down. Now, again, two up and one to the right brings you over to the other side, where the 12 is located. Just continue in this manner until all the squares are filled in. Now check the additions in illustration B. All 65s, right?

When you pick up the two cards, be sure to have the 6 in your right hand, the 5 in your left — so it will read 65 to your audience. Otherwise, they will be reading 56, which will certainly weaken the climax.

There are several important psychological factors involved in this presentation. Please follow the instructions, including the patter, to the letter.

The presentation of a Magic Square by itself is an interesting puzzle. By linking it with the cards we now have a magic effect. The Cut Force, as used in this trick, is a bold but simple way of forcing a card or cards on a spectator. It is one of many different methods. Most of the others involve a measure of sleight-of-hand. If you wish to progress with your conjuring you'll find these methods outlined in many different magic books. They're well worth learning.

The Three Cups

This is the trick I described earlier in this book — the one that puzzled a roomful of magicians in Montreal. The entertaining effect was originated by a magician named Bob Hummer. See if you can figure it out before you read the explanation.

What the audience sees: If you are in someone's home, ask the host to bring you three teacups. Place the cups, mouth down, in a row on a table top. Ask someone to crunch up a dollar bill into a small ball. Then demonstrate what she should do as you give verbal instructions. Point to each cup in turn, saying, "Each of these occupies a position," as you point to each from left to right. "This is position 1, this is position 2, and this is position 3. Now here's what you are to do. When I turn my back, place the little ball under any one of these cups. After that, change the position of the other two cups. In other words, if you put the ball under the middle cup (position 2) then you will change the position of the two end cups (the one in position 1 will go to position 3 and vice versa)."

Demonstrate this as you are speaking, so that the instructions are clear. Then continue, "Remember, there is no way I can know under which cup you placed the ball, or which cups you exchanged. Now, after you've done that you can change the positions of any two cups at a time by sliding them around — don't lift them; that may dislodge the ball. The only thing you must do now is to call out the position numbers that you are exchanging. For example, if you exchange the cups between positions 1 and 2, simple call out 'one and two' — if you are exchanging the end cups, call out 'one and three.' You can do this as many times as you wish —

just tell me when you've stopped."

Turn your back to the assistant and ask her to begin. When she announces "that's all" after calling out several moves, turn around and approach the cups. By this time the spectators will probably have lost track of which cup contains the ball. Put your hand to your forehead in deep concentration, say the appropriate words, and lift one of the cups. The ball will be under it!

How the trick is presented: The basic secret is a "key" cup. If you look at the outside bottom of almost any teacup you will see tiny marks or imperfections showing. When you place the cups down, mentally choose one of them which has a mark you can later identify. Remember its position. Now, when you turn your back, bring your right hand slightly forward so that it can't be seen by the audience, and use your fingertips as position markers. You do it in this manner: touch your thumbtip to the tip of your little finger — this is position 1. Touch your thumb to the next finger — this is position 2. The middle finger is position 3.

Start off by placing your thumbtip on the finger corresponding to the position of the key cup. Let us suppose it was position 3. Now, when the assistant starts calling out the positions being switched, follow along with your thumbtip whenever your number is called. For example, you started with your thumb on 3. If she calls "one and two," don't move your thumb. If she says "two and three," shift your thumb to position 2. If she then calls "one and two," move it to position 1 — and so on.

When the cup moving has stopped, make a mental note of the last position you held. Suppose it was 2. Turn around and, while you are acting out the concentration bit, look at the cups. If your key cup is in position 2, that's where the ball is. If one of the other cups is in position 2, then the ball is under the other non-key cup. That is all there is to it. And this is one trick you can repeat as many times as your audience would like, without any chance of the method being detected.

For the casual magician who wishes to do a stunning effect requiring no prior preparation, this clever trick is a natural.

12
Magical Presentation

A mateur magicians who are new at the game are usually very enthusiastic about their new-found powers. Their pockets stuffed with magical paraphernalia, they will often launch into a performance at the slightest provocation. As a performer you must realize that the onlooker isn't always as interested in your miracles as you are. I'm sure you have at one time or another attended a gathering where someone whipped out a deck of cards and zipped off sixteen astonishing tricks, nonstop — later to look up and find half the audience had vanished.

Caution is called for. If you must do a trick, do *one*, and do it well — a teaser. If someone asks, "How did you do that?" you've got them hooked. Just smile, and proceed to manufacture two or three more miracles. Then quit while you're ahead even if they get down on their knees and plead for more. There will be other times and other opportunities to display your prowess. I know it's not easy to do this, but believe me, it's worth it. It's much better to have your audience ask for more than to watch them drift away in the middle of your act!

And it shouldn't be necessary to remind you not to reveal the methods involved. You will often be pressed to do this, particularly by close friends. If you do, you will be knocking the props out from under your presentation. Tell them how it's done and you will usually hear, "Oh, is that all there is to it?" And you will also be going against the ethics of an honorable profession. Magicians themselves, when fooled by another magician, will never ask how it was done. It just ain't cricket.

Another important point: too many amateur conjurers present

their magical effects as puzzles. When this happens the audience will not guess the secret, but, at the same time, they will often be bored. If you want to challenge someone's intellect with a mathematical or logical puzzle, fair enough. But if you are presenting conjuring as an entertainment, that's what you should be doing — entertaining.

There are many ways to make your presentations entertaining. I personally have found humor to be a powerful ally. Get your audience laughing, and you have accomplished two things. First, they are relaxed and enjoying themselves. Second, they will be offguard at the crucial moment when you have to accomplish some deceptive hanky panky. I cannot instruct you on the use of humor. What works best for me is a tongue-in-cheek approach to my deceptions. You must use the kind of humor that suits your own personality.

If you are more comfortable with a serious approach, that too can be done. In that case, play the part of the magician who creates miracles. But above all, don't challenge your audience by adopting an "I am smarter than you" attitude. It just creates a no-win situation.

Whether you walk out on a stage or walk into someone's living room, if you are going to perform, the first thing you must do is to get the audience to like you and to relax, feeling that you are in charge of the situation. You are then off to a good start.

Routining is of great importance. This refers to the order in which you are going to present your tricks. One effect should lead smoothly into the other. Even if you are performing for an intimate group, you should have clear in your mind the order in which you plan to do your effects. To your audience it may seem like an impromptu little show, but in your own mind everything should be well planned. So if you want to appear to be pulling the odd item nonchalantly out of your pockets, be certain that you know in advance where each article is located!

I cannot stress strongly enough how important it is to practise each effect thoroughly. Magic must be perfection. Some tricks which look simple on paper (and there are several in this book) still need to be practised until they become second nature. You see, as every professional conjurer knows, the actual physical effects have to be done almost automatically, so that you can concentrate on what you are saying and how the audience is reacting. *That* is the big difference between a magician and a trickster.

And about the word "tricks." I'm constantly using the word in this book in order to get my message across. But I almost never use it where the public is concerned. Never refer to "tricks" when you are entertaining an audience. Call them anything else: effects; miracles; demonstrations. Try to avoid the connotation of "trickery." It's a psychological downer.

Now, as a magician, you have a lot of ammunition up your sleeve, if you will pardon the expression. There are many different ways to accomplish different effects. Let's take card tricks, for example. You can learn to use sleight-of-hand to maneuver cards secretly into different locations. Or you can use gimmicked apparatus. In the case of cards, it could be faked cards, such as cards with double faces or double backs. There are any number of trick decks on the market. The famous Svengali deck has been pitched at fairs and carnivals for years. With the Svengali you can perform astounding effects. Whole books have been written on this deck alone.

In the case of coins, the same conditions apply. Learn sleight-of-hand, or buy tricked coins. Yes, gimmicked coins do exist. Books have also been written about their use.

My advice? Learn sleight-of-hand with cards and coins. Why? Once you have mastered these manipulations you have a very strong ally — one you will never lose. Go anywhere, borrow a pack of cards or a few coins, and you're a magician. And you will have the pleasure that comes with mastering a skill which, let's face it, not many people possess. None of this rules out the use of gimmicked apparatus now and then, because if you combine dexterity with tricked articles, you now have even more control over your weaponry.

Although digital dexterity and gimmickry are essential, one other conjuring principle is really the most important of all — misdirection. Entire books have been written on magical misdirection, but I'll try to summarize the technique for you here.

One of the best books on the subject is *Magic by Misdirection* , written by Dariel Fitzkee, and published by Saint Raphael House in 1945. Fitzkee writes, "The true skill of the magician is in the skill he exhibits in influencing the spectator's mind." This skill is demonstrated by the manner in which the magician acts his part. His every word, his every gesture must be designed to mislead the spectator's thoughts. The performer places an Ace of Spades on top of a deck of cards. He then pretends to lift it off the deck but surreptitiously substitutes a deuce for the ace. Sliding the face-down deuce into the middle of the pack, he says, "Now keep your eye on the ace." This reinforces the spectator's belief that the ace has been shoved into the deck. This is a form of psychological misdirection which is repeated in many different ways during a performance.

Then there is physical misdirection, which also assumes many different forms. The magician gestures with his right hand while his left hand is performing the dirty work. Or, when doing a trick one on one, he makes eye contact for a moment with the unsuspecting spectator while his hands are making a quick move that must be covered in some manner.

On the stage, some bold actions have been covered up by some of the greatest magicians in front of a thousand people, using physical misdirection. Blackstone would actually exchange articles onstage for other articles slid out from the wings, right in front of an audience — while an assistant tripped and fell on the other side of the stage.

Misdirection means controlling the spectator's attention. Another way of doing this is through repetition. Let us say you have a small ball in your right hand. You want the spectator to believe you have placed it into your left hand, while you secretly retain it in your right. The actual move is to bring your hands together, tilt your right hand over your left (which would seem to make the ball drop into your left hand) and close your left fist, but secretly palm the ball in your right hand.

Fairly simple, isn't it? The spectator will believe it is in the left hand. Maybe. Let's look at the proper way to do it. Before you make the "move," actually do what you are supposed to be doing. As you are speaking, *do* drop the ball into the left hand. Toss it back to the right hand then drop it into the left again. You are evidently toying with the ball as you are speaking. The third time, do the actual move. We're not finished yet. Another important point: do *not* pull your right hand (with the concealed ball) back.

Move your left hand (apparently holding the ball) to the left. The spectator's attention will always be directed to the moving hand. And you do not want to draw attention to the hand that is concealing the ball. At the same time your patter, whatever it is, will be reinforcing your physical actions.

Misdirecting the mind of the spectator can be accomplished by doing familiar gestures that cover up surreptitious moves. An excellent example is that practised by the great card expert John Scarne. He would have someone select a card from a deck, look at and remember it, place it back in the deck, and shuffle the cards. Scarne would then say, "Name your card." Let us say it was the Queen of Hearts. Scarne would ask the assistant to remove it from the deck. She would scan the deck in vain. The Queen had vanished. Scarne would then reach into his mouth — and pull out the selected card!

Here's how he did it: after the spectator placed the Queen back in the deck, he would control the card to the top of the pack by using sleight-of-hand, then palm it into his right hand. Handing the cards to the assistant, he would ask her to shuffle them. While everyone's attention was on the deck being shuffled, Scarne would fold the hidden card in his hand in half and then in half again. Now, here's the real secret. Scarne was an inveterate cigar smoker. He almost always had a lighted cigar in his hand, bringing it to his mouth regularly for a few puffs. He would have the cigar in his mouth while folding the palmed card. Then, as he removed the cigar with his right hand, as he had been doing repeatedly, he simply slid the now folded card into his mouth. Everything was perfectly natural. The misdirection was perfect — everyone's attention was on the shuffling of the cards, and the move to his mouth was covered by his removal of the cigar.

I don't recommend that you adopt cigar smoking in order to become adept at the art of magic. But there are many other natural gestures that can be used to misdirect an audience's attention.

These are just a few brief examples of the detailed misdirection required in the performance of good magic.

At the same time the magician must never direct the audience toward anything which might arouse suspicion. This is a common beginners' error, which I have called "wrong direction." It goes something like this: the magician is using a trick deck of cards which look perfectly normal. He picks up the deck and says, "I have here a normal deck of cards." Or he holds up a transparent glass tumbler which has a false bottom concealing some milk, and he says, "As you can see, I'm holding an empty glass." In the first instance, there's no need to stress the word "normal." What else would a deck of cards be but normal? In the second case, it's redundant to announce that he is holding a glass — it's there for all to see. And it is quite evidently empty. In both cases he is planting a subconscious suspicion in the mind of the spectator.

Proper presentation of magic is impossible without proper rehearsal, whether for a theater performance or a fifteen-minute entertainment in a living room. Suppose you are going to present five tricks in your little fifteen-minute act. Each effect should be practised thoroughly by itself. Then the entire routine should be rehearsed, including the patter, as a whole. Now I know that sounds a little tedious for the casual amateur, but it's the only way you're going to make a good impression. There are no shortcuts.

If you progress to the point where you are practising sleight-of-hand, you'll find yourself surveying your moves in front of a mirror. This is fine. You must see your hands from the audience's viewpoint. And you should always check out how the manipulations look from various angles — the spectators are not always directly in front of you. A hinged, three-section mirror is very useful for this purpose.

But, a word of warning. Don't become too dependent on a mirror. You'll become "mirror-conscious" and will feel uneasy when performing without it. So just use your mirror to verify your moves at the beginning, then forget about it.

Doing a magic trick is like telling a good joke. Don't telegraph the punchline. If the spectator knows what the climax of the trick will be, he is more likely to spot the method that brought it about. Which is one reason why you should never repeat a trick for the same audience. Anticipating the climax, they will really be looking for the modus operandi.

There are two ways of taking advantage of this situation. If you can employ a different method to accomplish the same effect — and this can often be done — do so. Or if you can appear to be doing the same trick but end up with a different climax, you will definitely have your audience stumped. In other words, once you gain some experience, you can take advantage of every opportunity to make a strong impression. And you should always aim for a punchy surprise ending — it's not only deceptive, it's good theater.

Although it's usually bad magic to repeat a trick, it is often good magic to repeat an effect *within* a trick. Two classic examples come to mind. One is the card trick called The Ambitious Card, the effect being that the magician keeps sliding a card into the middle of a pack, and it keeps returning to the top. The more it is repeated the spookier it becomes.

The other effect is the classic Miser's Dream. This is the effect where the conjurer keeps pulling coins out of thin air and tossing them into a small pail. Producing one coin is a surprise — making dozens of them materialize is magic.

Learn these lessons well — then call yourself a magician!